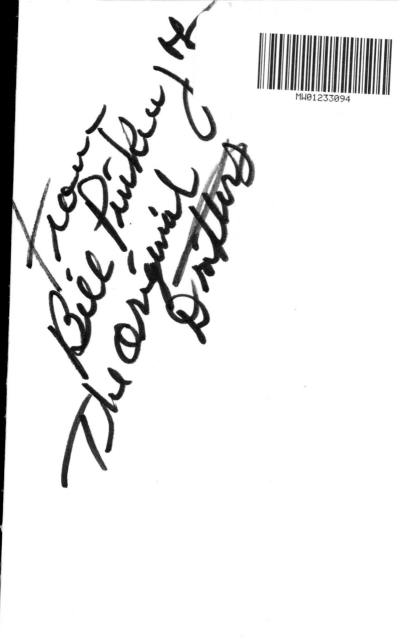

From
Bill Pink(?)
The Original
Brothers

DRIFTERS 1 :
BILL PINKNEY

CELEBRATING 50 YEARS
1953-2003

Bill Pinkney

As told to

Maxine Porter

**FIFTIETH ANNIVERSARY
COLLECTOR'S EDITION**

ISBN 0-9743953-1-5
Library of Congress Control Number: 2003099038

Published & Distributed By:
BillMax Publishing,
A division of
ORIGINAL DRIFTERS, INC
P.O. Box 371371
Las Vegas, NV 89137
www.originaldrifters.com

Also available in paperback
www.Drifters1.com
ISBN: 0-9743953-0-7

Layout & Design:
BEGINNING II END PUBLISHING
800 N. Rainbow, Ste. 208
Las Veags, NV 89107

DEDICATION

*I especially dedicate this writing
to the memory of my parents,
Murry and Katie Smith Pinkney.*

*I dedicate it further to
my family, my friends, my fans,
and my supporters over the years.*

TABLE OF CONTENTS

Prologues
Psalm 23

BILL PINKNEY
A ROCK AND ROLL LEGEND!

Although Alan Freed is credited with giving Rock 'n Roll its name, it was the early Drifters that gave it Heart and Soul. Bill Pinkney's style of the rolling bass in the harmony of the early records had never been done before. He influenced hundreds of singers and performers that would follow in the years to come.

Years ago when I spent time with Bill on the Rock 'n Roll tours, I realized that when Bill appeared on stage and sang, it felt like electricity in the room. I would watch the audience with great interest, and the excitement not only was on their faces, but it was in the air. We knew that we were in the presence of a very special performer, someone who comes along only once in a lifetime.

His combination of soul, rock 'n roll, gospel, and blues takes an ordinary tune and turns it into a revelation. You don't listen to a Bill Pinkney song. You drink it. It comes into your body like a breath of fresh air. You find yourself singing along from the second pew at the church, to hearing the salacious sounds of the blues drifting down the streets of Harlem.

In this business called Rock 'n Roll, many performers will find themselves nothing more than a footnote. But Bill Pinkney and The Original Drifters will live on into perpetuity.

For many of us in the music business, Bill Pinkney will always be the "Rock" in Rock 'n Roll. I am very proud to call Bill my friend.

Tony Belmont

Tony Belmont
PRESIDENT
Alan Freed Productions

Dear Bill Pinkney,

It is hard to believe that I would be writing about a person that I have known since my mid-teen years.

I can remember taking a short walk from my Father's luncheonette on 119th Street to 125th Street to the Apollo Theater to see all of the great singers. I am happy to say that I cannot count the times that I have seen The Drifters, watching them from the top of the balcony and enjoying every note they sang. Even at that age, I knew I was hearing one of the best groups around – a group that could bring tears, no matter who was doing the lead.

One of the reasons The Drifters has such a strong sound was that cool deep bass voice of Bill Pinkney, along with Bubba Thrasher, Gerhardt Thrasher, and the great Clyde McPhatter. The same Bill Pinkney who still travels the world with his Original Drifters, the same Bill Pinkney who decided to make me his lifetime friend, the same Bill Pinkney who makes me forever proud to have been a Drifter, and to be nothing but a true Drifter in my heart.

A Pal forever,

Ben E. King

Psalm 23

The Lord is my Shepherd;
I shall not want.

He maketh me to lie down in green pastures;
He leadeth me beside the still waters.
He restoreth my soul;
He leadeth me in the path of righteousness
For His names sake.

Yea, though I walk through
The valley of the shadow of death,
I will fear no evil
For Thou are with me;
Thy rod and Thy staff, they comfort me.

Thou preparest a table before me
In the presence of mine enemies;
Thou anointest my head with oil;
My cup runneth over.
Surely goodness and mercy shall follow me
All the days of my life;
And I will dwell in the house of the Lord
Forever.

This is my story,

This is my song.

Bill Pinkney

CHAPTER 1
A TIME TO REFLECT

When they called my name after a touching and beautiful introduction, I rose from my front row seat and headed for the stage, as I had done thousands of times in my more than four decades on the road. My sister Eliza was sitting to my right and my manager / partner Maxine was sitting to my left. My brother Henry, my son Darryl, four of my daughters, my niece Helen, my entire touring group, and many other supporters and friends were in the audience. As I walked up the steps onto the stage, I could feel myself getting very, very full.

When I did reach the podium, all I could do was hold on to it. I was completely overcome and I burst into tears. I was aware that the press camera lights began to flash everywhere, but I just cried. The color pictures were on the front page of the newspapers the next day.

It was the Inaugural Induction Ceremony on October 3, 1998 at the Vocal Group Hall of Fame and Museum, the brainchild of Tony Butala, an original singer with The Lettermen, and businessman James E. Winner, Jr.

The Original Drifters had been voted into its first class of inductees. The induction was a highlight of my professional career because it acknowledged how meaningful The Original Drifters' contributions were when we established the foundation upon which The Drifters' legacy was built. It represented so many experiences and so many people - singers, songwriters, producers, arrangers, engineers, fans, supporting family, and friends – who played a part over many years.

Renowned radio disc jockey Jack "The Rapper" Gibson, my long time supporter and friend who had played our records in the 1950s, had flown in from Las Vegas, Nevada just to present my award. To me, that was a real honor.

Our friend Peter Allman, from Celebrity Scene News, joined Jack for the trip from Las Vegas. Laverne Washington, from the Rhythm & Blues Foundation, had sent a touching congratulatory letter.

I composed myself and began to speak. "I stand here today on behalf of Clyde McPhatter, the organizer of The Drifters, Gerhardt Thrasher, Andrew Thrasher, and myself, Bill Pinkney. They are all gone now. But I'm still here. There have been many, many Drifters over the years, but we started it all. We were the foundation. We were the roots. And I have spent the last forty-five years of my life working to keep alive the sounds that we created back in 1953. I am so very thankful that God has left me here long enough to 'smell the flowers'."

It was a tremendous reunion of artists, representatives, and friends. I saw people that I had not seen for years. Now we had a chance to be together again. We were deeply moved by what was taking place.

VOCAL GROUP HALL OF FAME BREAKFAST WITH MY FAMILY

The fourteen groups inducted as The Inaugural Class and the people who represented them follow.

Pioneers of Musical Style	Charter Inductees
The Ames Brothers (Ed Ames)	The Original Drifters (Bill Pinkney)
The Andrews Sisters (Bob Boyer for Patty A.)	The Platters (Joe Terry)
The Boswell Sisters (Chica Minnerly - Vet's dtr)	The Supremes *(Mary Wilson / Pat Benti)
The Five Blind Boys Of Mississippi	The Beach Boys (Al Jardine)
Golden Gate Quartet	Manhattan Transfer (Tim Hauser)
The Mills Brothers (Donald Mills, Jr.)	Crosby, Stills, & Nash (not represented)
The Ravens (Warren "Birdland" Suttles)	

*Mary Wilson could not attend to accept for The Supremes. Since she was performing at Caesar's Palace in Las Vegas, my manager Maxine, who lives there, arranged for Motown personality Johnny Pate to go to Caesar's to present her award to her there.

Following the induction ceremony, we enjoyed a private reception, met with the press, and toured the impressive museum. It is a part of the ongoing downtown revitalization of Sharon, Pennsylvania, located about halfway between Cleveland and Pittsburgh. It features special exhibits, research material, old videos, music, a concert facility, and a gift shop. I urge all of my friends to visit there and recognize this great resource about vocal groups. All nostalgia music lovers should see it.

We all loved Linda Stewart-Savach, the efficient and dedicated Executive Director. Along with the help of her assistant Elaine Bell, Jim's daughter Karen Winner-Hale, and Jim's secretary Pam McKoy, she handled every detail to make sure that everyone in attendance had a memorable weekend.

My present group, The Original Drifters, was invited to headline the first annual Induction Concert on the next night at Montemurro's in Pittsburgh. The Lettermen, The Four Dots, and Johnny Angel & The Halos (tribute group led by VGHOF board member Jack Hunt) all performed. Original bassman Freddie Johnson with The Marcels and

Danny and the Juniors (featuring Joe Terry) made guest appearances.

The audience was one of the most receptive I have ever seen. I could feel the love and respect in the room as I worked my way through the audience singing. I will never forget that weekend.

This emotional time sent me into a mode of reflection. I looked back. You see, God had watched over me through many lives.

CHAPTER 2
GROWING UP IN SOUTH CAROLINA

I lived a typical southern childhood with the usual church upbringing in Dalzell, Sumter County, South Carolina. I was the second child of Murry and Katie Smith Pinkney. Daddy was an auto mechanic. Mama tended to the house and children, and sometimes picked cotton.

I was told that Mama left out of the field and went home to give birth to me. The midwife was Miss Swinton. I can remember as a child being in the field with her. I also can remember her beautiful singing voice well. She was the church Choir Leader. During the Depression, Mama used to wrap my feet with cloth from old Kroger sacks to keep the hot dirt from burning them. I think that I acquired my spirit of kindness and my freehearted nature from her. She was always able to feed somebody else by the Grace of God.

KATIE SMITH PINKNEY

MURRY PINKNEY, SR.

Dad was a great auto mechanic. He worked for Mr. Ben Carlisle, along with John Radfield (Mr. Benny Radfield's son) and Clyde Colclough.

Daddy kept us "in line" the old fashioned way. If we did wrong, he would send us outside to get a switch to whoop our butts. We used to call them "gum switches" because they would buckle, not break, and wrap around you and stick. We thought it was wrong then, but we learned later that discipline helped make us something.

We had a big and close family. I never knew my great-grandfather, Washington Pinkney, but I knew my grand-father, "Wash". Dad had six brothers, James (Donie), Fred, Arthur, Bernie, Benny, and George (Nossie), and three sisters, Delia Abram, Sadie Pinkney, and Rosa Pinkney. Aunt Delia lived to be 99. Mama had three brothers, Willie, Sam, and Jack, and five sisters, Beatrice Boykin, Lucy White, Eliza Jackson, Emma Washington, and Lessie Faulkner. I had lots of cousins.

My big brother Murry, 2½ years older than me, used to chop logs. I had a little bag to collect the chips that we used to start fires. One day when I was about five, I reached down to pick up some chips. My brother acci-dentally hit me in the head with the ax. Dad and Uncle Donnie rushed me over to Dr. Bush McLaughlin.

He shaved my head, rinsed it, and stitched it together. When I got back home, Mama rinsed it with kerosene, packed it with spider web, and tied my head back up. It could have been worse. At least I didn't have to face Mama's remedy for the mumps on that day. She would boil fat back or sardines; then she made it into a paste and put it around our necks. They didn't have hospitals for us.

A typical southern boy, I went bird hunting with a sling-shot. In the winter we would build traps in the snow and bait them with corn meal or husks. We would wait until a bird went in, and we would pull the string. Yes, we would eat them – fried, smothered, or in a stew.

I was the water boy for my big brother. He plowed an old mule from sunup to sundown for 50 cents a day. When it got too hot for the mule, my brother would take him up by the farmer's house to rest in the shade. We would go into the barn and shell corn.

I went to Ebenezer School in Dalzell, SC, the same school my Dad had attended, and my teachers all were Col-ored. In our one room school, we all started with books called Primers, and then went to Catechisms. It was like Head Start today. We started the first grade with Blue Backs. It seemed like all of the stories had cats and dogs in them. Frank Williams, Sr. (Bo) and I were great friends and we used to help each other in class. He usually knew the answer if I didn't.

The first people I remember were Rev. Miles Jackson and his wife, Mrs. Jackson. They had two daughters, Lanell and Sarah Belle, and two sons, Moses and Beacher. Miss Irick was my first teacher. Some of my other teachers were Miss Abraham, Miss Mabel Colclough, Mr. Titus Hastie (he taught me how to pitch a baseball), Professor Thompson, and Mr. Bracey. It was Mr. Bracey who told me "one day you are going to be something in athletics or entertainment".

I tried putting my Sunday suit in my book bag when I left for the two mile walk to school. I would stop in the swamp and change clothes. That lasted about as long as it took for my teacher to tell Mama how good I always looked in school. I got in big trouble about that.

Dr. McLaughlin's family sold my Dad a piece of land for thirty-five dollars. It was about a quarter of a mile down the road from the house where I was born. Mr. Benny Raffield and Mr. Elec Anderson, Sr. built our house there in 1934.

After our family moved, Mrs. Marie Johnson would pick me up at home and take me to school with her.

I loved to climb things. I fractured my collarbone when I fell out of a cherry tree when I was about seven. You can still see a slight sign of it today if you look closely.

Our family was growing. I had two sisters, Eliza and Bessie. My brother Henry and sister Jackie came later. Both of my parents had their own cars. Dad had two Fords – a Model T and a convertible. Later they got a '28 Chevy, a '31 Chevy, a '37 Chevy, and a '41 Ford.

When I was about thirteen or fourteen, I picked cotton for thirty cents per one hundred pounds. I wasn't too good at that though. We tried to think of some way to make the bag heavier. We would put some cotton bowls in the bag, or we would pour water or dirt on the cotton. Sometimes we got caught, sometimes we didn't. Picking cotton is how I earned the money to get my first bicycle, a Western Flyer. In 1940, I worked construction for thirty cents an hour.

My sister Eliza recently recalled:

"I remember when we got our first radio in the late '30's. We were listening to the Golden Gate

Quartet, and Bill said 'One day I'm going to sing on the radio!' All of us kids laughed. Our Dad said 'You must be going to *stand* on the radio and sing'. Bill's life teaches us to never take lightly a person's dreams and desires."

BILL'S CHILDHOOD PHOTO

- - - - - -

I was active and I really enjoyed singing and sports. I had grown up to be a strong willed teenager with my own ideas of how things should be done. I wanted to have my own way. It was time to leave home.

CHAPTER 3
DUTY CALLS

With the blessings of my parents, I enlisted voluntarily into the United States Army at the age of 17 in April, 1943 at Fort Jackson, Columbia, SC. It was during World War II when patriotic Americans everywhere were answering the call to defend our country. My serial number was 34655517. Charlie Mickens and I started and went all they way through together. I met Berkley Porter from Jonesville, SC, and Columbia, SC residents Bobby Simmons and John H. Johnson. I also met Ivory Perry there. I still see Charlie often now and talk to Berkley on the phone occasionally.

We were sent to Ft. Bragg, NC and from there to Camp Robinson near Little Rock, AR for our basic training. Corporal Richard Buford was from Louisville, KY and Corporal Smith was from Pittsburgh, PA. Marcus A. Poochie,

Guy A. Bernardo, James C. Williamson, Oscar E. Means, and John P. Ruby were the Lieutenants.

Fred Dozier, Jack Washington, and Garland Roy lead the 1st, 2nd, and 3rd Platoons. Berkley had the first section of our Platoon, and Sidney Jackson had the other. Our Sergeants were Clinton E. Sarras, Evans, Eugene S. Giddel, Hoyle McSwain (Biloxi, MS), and John M. Smith. Others were Captain Roland R. Perkins, Supply Sergeant Claude C. Plunkett, Sgt. Lark (Kansas City), Hack Martin (Washington, DC), Murphy Collier, Jack Robinson, and Corporal Jiggs Jones. Bill Hardy was the Company Clerk, and our nickname for his assistant Richardson was "Shorty".

We were called out to dig trenches after the big flood in 1943. Because the Colored military men were not allowed in downtown Little Rock, Spivey would drive the truck and take us to the USO Club on 9th Street every weekend. Spivey sometimes played drums at the club.

We formed The U.S. Friendly Five at Camp Robinson. Murphy Collier and George Simmons both sang lead tenor, Berkley Porter sang bass, Howard Smith sang baritone, and I sang on lead and baritone. Howard was a barber who was from Dothan, Alabama. He used to cut our hair.

We were a gospel group, and we would sing around at different churches in Gold Hill, Russelville, Clarksville, and Pottsville while we were on flood detail near Hot Springs. We went into Little Rock on the back of a 6x6 truck to sing with some other gospel groups. When they judged by applause, we won; when they judged by the most money raised, we won.

U.S. FRIENDLY FIVE

After five months, I received a furlough home, but it did not last long. I was called back to duty after five days. The 519th Regiment left Little Rock still in battalion. We were shipped immediately to Camp Miles Standish in Torrington, Massachusetts.

We boarded the *U.S.S. Explorer*, a freightliner, and crossed the Atlantic Ocean to Scotland. From there we went to Monemo in Northern Ireland, on to South Hampton and then to Liverpool in England. We crossed the English Channel on July 3, 1943 just after D-Day (D+6) during the Normandy invasion, and landed in France on the 4th of July.

We were a part of the European Theater of Operations 3rd Army Division, Quartermaster, Red Ball Express, 3991st Regiment, 135th Battalion. We were the Company L, DS service, detachment 101st Airborne ground transportation.

We dug our own foxholes and got in them. I can still remember wondering if I would ever get out of some of them alive. As bullets flew and bombs burst, we saw comrades fall. We saw some of them lose limbs. We saw some of them die. And we had to move forward.

BILL PINKNEY
U.S. ARMY - 1943

WORLD WAR II ARMY MEDALS

SGT. BERKLEY PORTER
NORTHERN FRANCE

It was a segregated Army then, and Coloreds were on the front line. Movies and television accounts don't tell it the way it really was. It was much later (in July of 1948) that President Harry Truman issued the Executive Order No. 9981 that directed "equality of treatment and opportunity" in the armed forces.

Our comrade Claude J. Marcey was killed in a Jeep wreck when he was thrown from his vehicle and hit his head on a tree stump just before his scheduled return home. A lot of us didn't make it back home alive. I made it through with just a frostbitten right foot.

I was good friends with the Wascott family in Swasone, France. Their children – Louis, Raymond, Jeanine, and Marcelle – were ages 10-17.

I sent a letter my Pastor, Rev. Fordham at Mt. Olive A.M.E. Church, asking the choir to sing "I Need Thee Ev'ry Hour". My parents both thought I had gotten killed because they had not received a letter in over a year, and the last one they got was defaced. I learned later that Mama passed out in church when she heard the letter read.

I made fifty dollars a month at first, then it went up to about eighty, and I sent a monthly allotment to Mama.

I helped put my sister Eliza through school. She retired from teaching in 1998. I'm proud of that.

I returned to the United States on the U.S.S. *George Washington* to Camp Kilmer, NJ. "Sentimental Journey" was playing when we sailed into the New York Harbor and saw the Statue of Liberty. It was good to be back in the United States. I went from there back to Ft. Bragg.

I was honorably discharged unharmed on December 27, 1945 with the rank of Corporal T-5. I was decorated with a Presidential Citation with four Bronze Stars for the following battles:

Normandy
Bastone (Ardeends, Battle of the Bulge)
Northern France
Rhineland

I also received a Rifle Marksmanship Medal, a Good Conduct Medal, and the Victory Medal. President Franklin Roosevelt ordered the citation, but President Truman issued it after Roosevelt's death.

You think about how important family and home are when you are away at war. When I was discharged, I decided to go home.

CPL. BILL PINKNEY

3991 TAKES THREE BASEBALL TITLE

The pennant race in the 135th Q. M. Bn. was sewed up by the 91st as they took two league games last week. They defeated the 3682 by the lopsided score of 11 to 2, and squeezed out a 6-5 win over 3419.

The league, with four teams, has completed almost all of its schedule, and there has been some red-hot competition. So far, the 3991 has not lost a league game, and have lost only two games over the entire stretch. These were to the 230 Gen. Hospital.

On Wednesday evening, the 91st avenged their two defeats at the hands of the medics when they blanked them with a tally of 5-0.

3991 Q.M. DRIVER

The Distinguished Unit action of the Presidential Citation for service during the siege of Bastogne was presented to all the drivers and some of the mechanics of the 3991 QM Truck Co. at ceremonies recently held in the company area.

Lt. Col. Hinkle, the battalion C. O. presented the awards, and the citation was read by Capt. Perkins, the 3991 Company Commander.

In addition to the unit citation, 15 drivers were awarded drivers medals These medals are granted for proficiency in driving over a certain period of time, and are prized possessions of the men who received them.

With full ceremony, presentation of arms etc. the Presidential Citation Authority was read, and each of the officers and drivers were given his gold edged blue ribbon to wear on his uniform. As the badges were given out, many remembered their experiences as they helped the 101 Airborne in Bastogne.

The 3991, among others helped to carry the 101 Airborne men to Bastogne, and were caught in the Ardennes offensive, more commonly known as "The Bulge". The valor of all in that area is a well known story and need not be related here. It is sufficient to say that they all did fine jobs, and they will remember the affair for a long time.

WINS "E" PENN

For being the best trucking in Ois. Section the 3991 truck co. was awarded the "E" Pennant for the month of June. Over five three trucks were inspected. This is the third company to receive the "E" Pennant on this depot.

CHAPTER 4
HOME AGAIN

I took the bus from Ft. Bragg back to Sumter, SC, and then took a taxi to Mr. Willie Black's house, my brother Murry's father in law. We got into his car and he drove me straight to my Dad's Murry Pinkney Grocery Store right next to our family home in Dalzell.

Mr. Black went inside the store and told Dad "I've got somebody out here I want you to see". "Lord have Mercy" was all that my Dad could say when he saw me. We embraced. We went immediately next door to our house. He told me to walk real close directly behind him so that nobody would see me coming.

Mama was sorting clothes when she looked up and saw me standing there. She let out a shout and then fell out. Dad had to get her up off the floor. My brother Murry, who recently had come home from the Navy, said "Oh, just look at you. You have grown so much". It was a joyful day.

I returned to Dalzell and settled into the typical southern lifestyle in the place where I grew up. Although I was a decorated war veteran, there was no heroes welcome. I just went home. That's the way it was in the 1940's south.

I drew $90.00 a month muster payment for three months and went to auto mechanic school under the G.I. Bill. I did some work as a tailor, and then I worked as an auto mechanic apprentice under my father for five dollars a day. Silas (Chookie) Abrahm and I worked side by side.

I was really trying to adjust to being home and making it there. A couple of years passed. I had gotten married, and my Dad had built us a house on the property. I got a Civil Service job at Shaw Air Force Base driving an Army 6 x 6 dump truck to haul the charcoal for the boilers that heated the barracks.

Eliza recalled when I recruited some cousins and friends and formed a gospel group called The Singing Cousins. We used to rehearse at the house and sing around at church functions. I enjoyed singing every chance I got.

THE SINGING COUSINS (L TO R): MATTHEW GALLASHAW, DAVID GLOVER, HERBERT GLOVER, JAMES MACK, BILL PINKNEY, AND WESLEY MACK

- - - - - -

In 1947, Rev. John Williams, Sr. founded a secret organization called the Twelve Tribes of Israel in Sumter County. My father and eleven other men were charter members. When Rev. Williams' son, John, Jr., got out of the service, he had gone to embalming school and wanted to start a business. The group, to support him, formed The Twelve Tribes Union Funeral Home in 1943. His father went to work with him and went to school too. There was a law later that no organization could own a private business. John, Jr.'s brother Frank Williams, Sr. bought the business and renamed it the Williams Funeral Home. The Twelve Tribes organization eventually disbanded.

Our families were so close that Frank, Sr.'s children didn't know I wasn't their real uncle until they had almost reached adulthood. They all still call me "Uncle Bill", and I'm still their Uncle.

ORIGINAL OFFICERS "TWELVE TRIBES UNION FUNERAL HOME," SUMTER, SC 1947. PRESENT NAME, WILLIAMS FUNERAL HOME, INC. 1957-

TOP ROW (L TO R): REV. JOHN W. WILLIAMS, JR., MR. ROBERT ANDERSON, REV. RICHARD LLOYD, MRS. MARTIN, MR. MURRY PINKNEY, SR. (BILL'S FATHER), MRS. JANETT GARNER.

BOTTOM ROW (L TO R): DEACON J.C. CAPTERS, REV R.H. DAVIS, REV. GABE TILLMON, B.J. CHESTNUT, REV. JOHN W. WILLIAMS, SR.

NOT IN PHOTO: REV. H.W. KIRK

But I just wasn't satisfied with the way my life was going. I had been away to war defending my country. I had seen other places, other things, and other countries. I wanted something more. In 1949, I decided to take my young wife on the train and move up north to New York to follow my dreams for greater opportunities – maybe in professional sports.

CHAPTER 5
NEW YORK, NEW OPPORTUNITIES

New York was like a different world. Colored folks up there seemed to be doing fine and living better than folks in the south. Since we got up there with almost no money, we lived with my wife's cousin Mozell Howard in a small room in the attic and I looked for a job.

I had never heard of the "numbers", but I took a chance. I played 495 and got a few hundred dollars to tide us over. I got a job at the Divego Sporting Goods store in Jamaica, LI and then at the Bermer Ribbon Company in Manhattan. Later I worked as a bellman and crank-style elevator operator at the Woodside Hotel. I served coffee to Billie Holiday's room. I also met Count Basie who later had a hit "Jumping at theWoodside."

I had time to pursue my special interests. In the evening after work, I played sandlot baseball. We started in Central Park. I was quite an athlete already. I worked my way into pitching for the New York Blue Sox sandlot team. I threw a mean slow sidearm curve. I remembered how my schoolteacher Mr. Hastie had taught me how to grip the ball to throw a fast or slow curve.

I had to leave baseball because I didn't want to be away from home traveling so much. I got a job at Ford Motor Company's Sutton Motors off East River Road near 96th. I detailed cars and was a mechanic's helper making twenty eight dollars a week.

I was starting to look toward my musical interest too. The Apollo Theater was well known for its shows and for its Talent Night at The Apollo. I went on and sang the Willie Mabon song "I Don't Know (What My Baby's Putting Down)".

A while later I went on again. The Lucky Millender Band was playing. When I went on stage, touched the Tree of Hope, and told the emcee my name and where I was from, you would have thought the whole theater was from South Carolina. I came in second place that night singing Sonny Til & The Orioles' "It's Too Soon To Know".

- - - - - -

I met Benjamin Peay in 1949 through Louis Jones, manager and lead singer of the gospel group The Jerusalem Stars. Ben became known later as Brook Benton professionally. He was from my home state in Lugoff near Camden, SC.

We became very good friends. In the evenings, we would sit outside on the stoop in front of where I lived at134th & Lenox in Harlem and talk about our lives and goals – whoever would make it first would help the other try to make it too. He was a great songwriter and we knew he would make it.

He was a "floater" with The Jerusalem Stars, someone who is in and out just doing some of the gigs. I started singing with them in 1950 and stayed roughly a year.

My fellow South Carolinian Willie Massey had left The Jerusalem Stars before I joined to found The Southern Knights with Alton Griffin, Herman Bailey, Doc Pearson, and Carl Hughes. Massey and Griffin replaced three members with Jimmy Powell, James Bryant, and me. I stayed with the group until November 1952.

Although I lost touch with Ben Peay for a while, we never lost our friendship.

Ben went on to sing in The Golden Gate Quartet with Bill Langford, who was known as "High Pocket", and kept writing songs. He wrote and sang so well that he would do demos and end up recording them himself. I am told that he actually wrote, "It's Just a Matter of Time" for Nat King Cole, but ended up making it a big hit for himself instead. He had some well remembered records - "So Many Ways", "The Boll Weevil Song", "Endlessly", and "Hotel Happiness. I liked his very first song, "A Million Miles From Nowhere". His recordings of "Baby You've Got What It Takes", and "That's A Rockin' Good Way" with Dinah Washington were both big hits too.

The Southern Knights would get together with other gospel groups for quartet singing in churches in New York City. We got the chance to go back to South Carolina for a gospel program. I was happy to get to go back to see my family and friends.

THE SOUTHERN KNIGHTS OF N.Y.C.

Eliza Pinkney Pearson recalls:

> "Bill came home from New York singing with the
> gospel group The Southern Knights. I was so
> pleased, because our Father got the chance to
> see Bill realizing his dream. Dad didn't live to
> know about The Drifters because he passed away
> during the following year from a massive heart
> attack."

- - - - - -

After we finished one of our gospel programs, I went to a small store- front church in Harlem to see the Mount Lebanon Gospel Singers.

Clyde McPhatter was the lead singer. He had a unique, clear, and unbelievably beautiful tenor voice. The other singers in the group were Charlie White, William "Chick" Anderson, David Baldwin (brother of author James Baldwin), and James "Wrinkle" Johnson. When the program was over, I met Clyde and talked with him for a while. I never would have dreamed on that day what an impact that voice would have on my life.

DOMINOES WITH CLYDE MCPHATTER (FAR LEFT)

DOMINOES WITH JACKIE WILSON (FAR RIGHT)

CHAPTER 6
HOW THE DRIFTERS GOT STARTED

Clyde had stopped singing with the gospel group and had been singing with Billy Ward and The Dominoes, leading hits including "Have Mercy, Mercy Baby", "Don't Leave Me This Way", "These Foolish Things Remind Me of You", "Deep Blue Sea", "The Bells". Folks used to call him "Clyde Ward, Billy's little brother", because it was his voice that really defined that group for the most part. Because Clyde and Billy Ward had differences, Clyde eventually left the group, and Jackie Wilson took his place.

Ahmet Ertegun, head of the upstart from Atlantic Recording Company, came to see a Dominoes show and asked where Clyde was. When he learned Clyde was gone, he got in touch with Clyde and told him that he wanted to form a new group with him.

In June of 1953, Gerhardt Thrasher came by and told me that Clyde was putting together a rhythm and blues group. He said Clyde already had tried one recording session at Atlantic with his gospel group doing "Gone", and "Lucille", but the company was not satisfied with the sound. They said the sound was too light, not balanced. They wanted some stronger voices – gospel anointed voices.

We got together at my house at 108 West 134th Street in Harlem, NY for our first rehearsal. Clyde was the lead, Andrew (Bubba) Thrasher was on tenor, Gerhardt (Gay) Thrasher was on baritone, and I was the top tenor. We rehearsed around at each other's houses. Sometimes we would rehearse at our friend Carrie's apartment because she was a great cook. She would bake chicken and turkey and feed us.

We all lived pretty close together. Clyde was on the west side of 127th near 7th Avenue, Gay and Bubba were on 128th, and I was at 134th and Lenox Avenue. The guys were all young, in their late teens and early twenties. I was the oldest, at twenty-seven, so Clyde put me in charge as the group Spokesperson.

Clyde was a nice young happy go lucky kid. His family had come to New York from Durham, NC in the 1940's. His father was Reverend Cecil McPhatter, a Pentecostal minister. I knew his older brother Thomas, his sisters, Gladys, Johnnie, and Louise, and his little brother Joe. That whole family could really sing.

Besides Clyde's great voice, he had good looks, winning ways, and a magnetic smile. Gay was the older and more serious Thrasher brother with a great, great tenor voice that reminded me of Beachy in The Dixie Hummingbirds. Bubba was a natural comedian. He had Jackie Gleason down pat. He also was a great emcee. They were from Wetumpka, Alabama.

Clyde added Willie Ferbee to the group to give it some bottom. When we auditioned for Atlantic, they loved us and set up rehearsals with arranger Jesse Stone. We went to 234 West 56th Street for our first recording session with the company on August 9, 1953. Company? It was a room. The desks and everything else were piled up in the corner to make enough room for us to record. The "company" was Ahmet Ertegun, Herb Abramson, and Jerry Wexler. Later Miriam Beinstock and Ahmet's brother Neshui came aboard.

We used two microphones. Clyde was at one mike and the rest of us were around the other one. Jesse Stone was our arranger and Tommy Dowd was our engineer.

They were ready for us, and we were ready for them. We hit those mikes full force. We recorded three songs – "Money Honey", "Let the Boogie Woogie Roll", and "The Way I Feel." Jesse wrote "Money Honey". They loved our recordings so much that they offered us individual contracts. Although Willie was on the first recording session with us, he left right after that and never toured with us. Clyde shuffled me to bass, Bubba to baritone, and Gay to tenor. That's how The Drifters ended up being a quartet.

Clyde already had signed with Atlantic. He had gotten out in May from under the contract he had with Federal Records from his days with The Dominoes. Tommy Dowd told me that he got the job of escorting Clyde over to Federal Records to get his contract release after some wheeling and dealing.

When we signed those individual contracts with Atlantic, we became the cornerstones in the foundation upon which The Drifters' legacy was subsequently built.

We really had just gotten it together. We didn't even have a name yet. Although it was true that all of the group members had drifted from one group to another, that is not how the group got its name.

I remember the question "What are we going to call our-selves". Clyde said, "Let's call ourselves "Drifters, The Drifters". Everyone liked it. That was that.

BILL PINKNEY, WILLIE FERBEE, CLYDE MCPHATTER, ANDREW THRASHER, AND GERHARDT THRASHER

I still hear from some of the children and other family members of our original group from time to time. It is always a pleasure.

- - - - -

Our first release was in September 1953. Three new acts were on the announcement flyer – Ray Charles ("Heartbreaker"), Laverne Baker ("Soul on Fire"), and us with "The Way I Feel" on the A side and "Money Honey" on the B side. Our first job was at a little club in Maryland near the DC line, and the next was in Atlanta. That was the start of my life on the road under "Drifters" banners.

BILLBOARD RELEASE PAGE

A radio disc jockey flipped over "The Way I Feel" and started playing "Money Honey", and it started getting some real attention. It got great reviews in the trades and was a "Pick of the Week" in early October.

All recording artists should give due credit to the radio disc jockeys. They are the ones who made hits out of record. No matter how good we were, if the deejays hadn't played our music, people couldn't hear it, and if they couldn't hear it, how could they buy our records?

We had a hit record! It was one of the biggest thrills of my life to turn the radio on and hear "Money Honey" playing for the first time. I said, "Hey, I'm on that! The big scream in the middle – that's me!" Even now, many people think that it was Clyde. But it was me.

"Money Honey" shot straight onto the charts and stayed there for three, almost four months. That really was a big accomplishment for a brand new act in 1953.

A few years later "Money Honey" was "covered" by Elvis Presley, just like he covered Big Willie Mae Thornton's "Hound Dog." Peggy Lee's cover of Little Willie John's "Fever" was another good example. That's what they called it when a white artist recorded something from R&B. Their records would be softer, more acceptable to mainstream radio. Ours showed that we all had gospel anointed voices. Let's face it, they didn't want colored faces on album covers.

Our first engagement at the Apollo Theater was in early October. Frank Schiffman was in charge and his son was named Bobby. Span and Roy were the back stage managers. They made sure we had our calls – thirty minutes, twenty minutes, ten minutes, and five minutes. We were on the show with George Shearing.

In November we appeared with the Bullmoose Jackson Orchestra for Alan Freed in Steubenville and Youngstown, Ohio. We played Alan's Harvest Moon Ball in Akron and at the Ebony Lounge in Cleveland.

Atlantic's management gave us a lot of attention. Ahmet was later quoted as having said "As far as we're concerned from the moment we sign an artist, they're already a star." He and Jerry spent some real time on us to help make that happen. They would bring us material, and Clyde would usually pick out the songs he liked and work out the harmony. Clyde had hand picked the singers and organized the group centered around his lead singing. It was our understanding that we all co-owned the group, but Clyde was the one who was "in charge" and I spoke for us.

Our first guitar player, Walter Adams, passed away. Then we had Ham, Chauncey, Jimmy "Goody", who traveled with us a lot, Jimmy Oliver, and Reggie Kimber.

- - - - - -

Clyde married Nora Lee in 1953. I heard that she eventually went blind. They didn't have any children. Bubba married Bea, and Gay was already married to Emma

- - - - - -

We went back into the "studio" in mid November and recorded "Such a Night", "Don't Dog Me", "Warm Your Heart", and "Bip Bam". The record company released "Such A Night" in January of '54. Although we didn't record "Lucille", they put it on the B side. That song came from Clyde's June, 1953 session with his gospel group. We went on to play a week at Howard Theater in Washington, DC, a week at the Royal Theater in Baltimore, and a week at the Regal Theater in Chicago.

Our next recording session in February 1954 produced "The Bells of St. Mary's", "Whatcha Gonna Do", "Honey Love", and the Irving Berlin classic "White Christmas". I sang the bass lead on "White Christmas", and Clyde sang the lead tenor. We wanted to do something different with "White Christmas". We did it in a ballad-with-a-beat version that became a big hit!

Atlantic wondered what composer Irving Berlin would think. He surprised everyone when he gave our version his blessings. He really liked it and he contacted Atlantic with a letter of congratulations.

CENTER LABEL AND FLYER - "WHITE CHRISTMAS"

Our "White Christmas" has been used in quite a few movies. "Home Alone", "The Santa Claus(e)", and "Mixed Nuts" are just some of the ones I heard about in the 1990's. Four decades after we made it, ABC TV's Good Morning America researched it to be in the top ten all time best selling holiday records. I am told that it is the all time best selling Drifters recording as well because of its annual appeal. It has been reissued many times and shows up on holiday compilations every year.

It sure would be nice to see some royalties since they used my voice on the "Home Alone" soundtrack. It was a blockbuster movie and is still a success in the home video market. My manager saw it on Delta Air Lines as an in-flight entertainment presentation in December, 2002.

- - - - - -

We were back in the studio in March recording "There You Go", "Try Try Baby", "If I Didn't Love You Like I Do", and "Someday You'll Want Me To Want You". I did the bass narration on "Someday...". "Money Honey" was still on the charts and "Such A Night" was on its way up. We all were happy. We thought we had "made it".

- - - - - -

We used the car I already had, a '47 Cadillac 4 Door Sedan 62 Series, for traveling from town to town. Clyde loved to drive, but he wasn't what you'd call a driver.

We were on our way to Atlanta, GA. Clyde was driving. He pulled into a service station, hit the gas pump, and dented the car. Actually, he hit the concrete around the gas pump. To tell you the truth, I wasn't as worried about my car as I was about that white man's gas pump. No damage. We gassed up and got away from there fast. I ended up giving that car to my brother-in-law.

We had a close call when we had car trouble while passing through Fredericksburg, VA. A group of fellows had just robbed a bank or a loan company. Our out of town Cadillac got the attention of the police. When they took us over there, no one could identify us as the robbers. We were standing there with our hands up like criminals.

They decided to search the car trunk for red clothing since one of the robbers was wearing red. When I put my hand down toward my pocket to get the keys, I made a big mistake. The officer hit his gun and said "Boy, good thing your hands went back up. You almost got it". I told him fast I was just reaching for the keys. Once they searched the car and found nothing red, we were all right. It took hours to get that car fixed and back on the road. We didn't want to see Fredericksburg again soon.

- - - - - -

Mildred Ward Coffey recalls:

"I met The Drifters when I was still in high school. Bill, Dave, Gay, and Bubba came to Kansas City a couple of times a year to perform. They struck up friendships with my older brothers, Leon and Vernon.

"Everyone enjoyed the shows. The group often visited Uncle Lonnie's home. They loved Aunt Cricket's home cooking, and she fed them just 'like family'. Over the years, our family has kept in contact with Bill."

- - - - - -

We were working with some great people in the business: Joe Glazier - Gale Agency, Ben Bart and Dick Allen - Universal Attractions, Frank Sands - Circle Attractions. Things seemed to be going fine for us.

I met Hank Ballard when he was singing tenor for The Royals. Henry was their lead singer. They soon had to change their name because it was too close to "The Five Royales". I also was good friends with The Spaniels – Pookie Hudson, Willie C., Earnest, Cortney, and Gerald.

Sam Cooke was a great guy. What a lot of folks don't know is that, when he first left The Soul Stirrers, he went out on the road with us considering joining The Drifters. His brother L.C. recently mentioned the time in 1954 when we performed in Chicago at the Parisian Hotel. He and Sam left with us for our next job in Wisconsin. He stayed on a while, but Sam decided to go back to The Soul Stirrers after about five days. When he left that group again for the last time, he went into a solo R&B career. I often include a medley of Sam's hits in my shows.

- - - - - -

When Dick Clark had his television show in Philadelphia, we were on it. In fact, I believe we were probably one of the first Black acts on the show. We also appeared on Alan Freed's TV show "The Big Beat".

Yes, things seemed to be going just fine. Then Clyde got drafted into the Army on May 7, 1954, exactly one year to the day after he signed with Atlantic. We were performing at the Royal Peacock in Atlanta when he got the news.

Although we never had any written agreements other than our individual recording contracts with Atlantic, Clyde's personal manager assumed some managing duties. I was the Road Manager, Spokesperson, and recruiter.

I still can still hear Clyde's voice telling me to keep it together, to keep it going. I remember the many times that I walked the streets of Harlem looking for singers. I had to, because I promised Clyde that I would.

CHAPTER 7
MOVING FORWARD

Atlantic released "Honey Love" and "Warm Your Heart" later in May. Clyde and Tommy Dowd wrote "Honey Love". Jerry Wexler and Jesse Stone did the arrangement. It was banned for its "suggestive lyrics". Its popularity and the demand for it was that much greater.

The Drifters (Gay, Bubba, and I only), under the name The Rhythmakers, sang background on Ruth Brown's "Oh What A Dream", "Somebody Touched Me", "Old Man River", and "Please Don't Freeze". You can really hear me on them too. Ruth had a number one hit that summer with "Oh What A Dream".

We recruited Dave Baughan to sing lead. I had to get his mother's permission for him to go out on the road because he was so young. Lucky for us, Clyde was stationed close enough that he still could do some of the jobs with us.

In fact, we recorded "Hot Ziggety", "Three Thirty Three", "Sugar Coated Kisses", and "Everyone's Laughing" with Clyde while he was on leave from the military.

The group, with Little Dave on lead, toured the Midwest with Billy Eckstine, Peggy Lee, and comedian George Kirby. Although Dave sounded a lot like Clyde and had the voice we needed, right from the start we had problems with him.

Atlantic released our "What'cha Gonna Do" and pulled the canned June 1953 "Gone" for the B side in 1955. Both sides became hits.

We were getting ready for a Feld six-week tour around the eastern half of the country with Laverne Baker, Roy Hamilton, Faye Adams, The Spaniels, The Clovers, King Pleasure, the Rusty Bryant Orchestra, and the Erskine Hawkins Orchestra. We set out with Little Dave on lead, but we knew it couldn't last.

- - - - - -

ANDREW THRASHER, BILL PINKNEY, JIMMY OLIVER, DAVID BAUGHAN, AND GERHARDT THRASHER

We were at the first tour stop in Cleveland, Ohio when Sonny Turner came to visit me at the Majestic Hotel. He was just a youngster and he had a local singing group. Sonny went on to become The Platters' second lead singer after Tony Williams. We keep in touch to this day and our groups sometimes perform together.

- - - - - -

The Drifters kept performing, and I was always on the look out for good singers. We went back to Cleveland to perform at the Circle Theater with Wilbert Harrison, Arthur Prysock, and the Paul Weston Orchestra. I was in the men's room and I overheard someone singing. He sounded very good, so I asked him if he was working. He said he was singing with a group called The Hornets. I asked him if he would be interested in singing with The Drifters. He said to me "Are you shitting me?" I told him no I wasn't, that Clyde had been drafted into the Army, and we needed a good, reliable lead singer. I told him to have his bags packed the next morning. I called the office and told them I had found a new lead singer. The young man from Selma, Alabama, Johnny Moore, left with us the next day.

We had two lead singers then, so Little Dave got his act straightened up. In fact, he did so well that Johnny left for a while. But it didn't last long. So we called Johnny back.

We were working in Chicago in 1954 when I met The Flamingos – Paul Wilson, "Little Johnny" Carter (who went on to be The Dells' well known tenor), Nate Nelson, and cousins Ezekiel and Jacob Carey. They were all great guys. I saw Zeke and Jake over the years, and often in the 90's when both groups had Vegas engagements at the same time.

When Clyde was discharged from the Army, we thought he would come back to The Drifters. But that did not happen. He told me that he liked what the group was doing and make sure I kept it going. He was going solo.

At the beginning of an Irvin Feld Tour, a '54 Eldorado convertible pulled up. It was so pretty it looked like it changed colors from aqua to burgundy. Fats Domino told me then "Hey Boy, one day you'll get one of these!"

"Snook" Fuller was the first one who brought us to the ABA Club in Greensboro, NC in 1954.

ALMA PINKNEY

I was a happily married young man with a daughter and another child on the way. My wife had been in Harlem Hospital at 135th and Lenox in labor for a couple of days.

We were performing at the Apollo Theater, New York City. After each show during the break I would get in my car and drive the few blocks to see about her. Mrs. Lottie Black, her mother, had come up from Carolina to be with us and to help with the new baby.

The last night when I got there, my wife was in delivery - in great pain. I could hear her saying "I'm dying. I'm dying". And I couldn't get to her. Then her voice stopped. A couple of minutes later, the doctors, nurses, and her mother came to me. They said, "She's gone". I said "Gone? Gone where? Did you move her somewhere?" They said, "She died". I had lost both my wife Alma and my first son during childbirth.

After my mother in law went back to Carolina, Willie and Rosalie Massey helped me with Eartha while I worked. But with my schedule, I soon accepted the fact that I had to take my two-year-old little girl back to South Carolina for her Mama's mother to raise.

How could everything just fall apart?

I put my all into my work.

- - - - - -

We were in Macon, Georgia working at the National Guard Amory in about 1955. Lacy Hollingsworth, my driver, told me between shows that there was some little fellow that kept bugging him about wanting to sing. He asked if I would call the guy up during the next show and let him do a song. It couldn't hurt, and Lacy said it would get the guy off his back. I welcomed the young man to the stage, as I do artists even today. Well this fellow got up there and really started moving, with showmanship and real potential. That young man went on to become very, very famous. He was James Brown.

I was living at the Teresa Hotel in New York in about '57 or '58. James came by there on the way to a show in Connecticut. I got into the 1955 Cadillac with him and his saxophone player JC Davis and rode up there with them for the show. When James first came out, his manager was Clint Brantley.

I spoke with James and crossed paths with him from time to time over the years. When I made a special trip to attend his 60th birthday party in Augusta, GA we talked about that night when we met in the fifties.

In September of '55 while touring in Los Angeles, Johnny, Bubba, Gay, and I recorded "Drifting Away From You", "Your Promise To Be Mine", "Ruby Baby", "Steamboat", and "Adorable". I arranged and sang the lead on "Steamboat". Maxwell Davis arranged the others. Gay and Jimmy wrote "Your Promise To Be Mine". Buck Ram, who went on to manage The Platters later, wrote "Adorable". The Colts had recorded it before us, but we made it a hit. Ours was used in a British TV commercial for Impulse body spray in 2002.

I saw The Pilgrim Travelers in Los Angeles. They all had '54 –'55 Cadillac Fleetwoods. I had already met Lou Rawls at the Apollo in New York through his manager Alexander.

In June, we were back in New York recording "Soldier of Fortune", "Honky Tonky", "Sadie My Lady", and "I Gotta Get Myself A Woman".

CHAPTER 8
THE ATLANTIC FAMILY

The Atlantic family of artists was just that – like a family of brothers and sisters. We spent so much time together with the same goal of wanting to make it big with our music.

Laverne Baker and Ruth Brown became the premiere female artists at Atlantic. Clyde McPhatter, Ray Charles, The Clovers, and blues man Joe Turner, Earl "Fatha" Hines, Ivory Joe Hunter, Chuck Willis, The Cardinals, and, of course, us – The Drifters - were on the roster. We all were cranking out R & B hits one after another.

Atlantic's management had us touring on many shows together in different combinations, and we developed many lasting friendships. Sometimes it got rough out there, but it was the life that we chose and we lived it.

Ruth Brown described it this way in her book:

> "One final compensation lay in the camaraderie among artists. We told jokes, played games, laughed, cheated, shot the bull and made love. That last was inevitable, for we were all flung in at the deep end of the adrenalin tank, and for up to ninety days at a time…traveling together, hanging out together, performing together…sometimes there was love together…and these little 'tingums' could be hot stuff while they lasted."

Clyde and Ruth weren't always exactly like brother and sister. In fact, they dated pretty heavy when he was in the service. It wasn't until over forty years later, even after her autobiography came out, that my old friend Ruth finally would acknowledge to the world that Clyde was her son Ron's biological father. But that's another story.

The artists were all young. Most of us were green about the business in general and few knew anything about the legal side of it – trademarks, copyrights, etc. We came up with song ideas, or arrangement changes, and other things that make a record or a show really successful and memorable to the public.

We thought we were doing good just to get paid and to be treated good at the venues. We didn't know about the potential for more income - that we had rights that could and should have been protected. When I wrote and arranged "I Should Have Done Right", I didn't get any credit for it. We all "learn(ed) the hard way".

People often refer to Atlantic as "The House That Ruth Brown Built". I don't want to take anything away from her because she did so much. But we did our part too.

RICHMOND, VA

CHAPTER 9
LIFE ON THE ROAD - THE 1950'S

We spent a lot of time on the road traveling from one job to another. We played in many clubs throughout the South on what was often called the "chittlin' circuit". We also did special events and parties.

Most of our travel was in private cars. There was no air conditioning in the cars then. It was terrible to have car trouble in the middle of nowhere in the heat, but we learned how to survive on the road. We had pots and pans and hot plates. Somebody, including me, always had some serious food going on in those rooming houses and motels. We had to do it, because racism was so common that we often would have trouble finding food. So we'd cook for ourselves.

Here's what Ruth Brown had to say about those days:

"Audiences apart, first and foremost for us on
those difficult but economically essential tours was
the music. That was the compensation. Most
good R-and-B musicians were not professionally
trained, and the way we played in these often dan-
gerous circumstances, well, there has to be a different kind of attitude when you look down and
observe the segregated curtain or clothesline
down the center of an auditorium or dance hall…

local people just waited for the music to come, and for those of us who brought it to their neighborhood - the Charles Browns, the Clovers, the Drifters, the Clyde McPhatters, the Coasters, the Jackie Wilsons, the Sam Cookes, the Fats Dominoes, the Little Richards. All these people, all these groups, with their great musicians, are the ones who suffered every sling and arrow the South had to offer in those days. It was for the sake of the music that we did it. And maybe we helped progress along a little."

I had the pleasure of meeting (Little) Richard Penniman in Macon, Georgia in the early fifties by handshake. I got to know him personally later when we played at the Broadway Capital Theater in Detroit.

I met The Moonglows - Harvey Fuqua, Prentiss Barnes, Bobby Lester, and Pete Graves - when we played at the Apollo in the early fifties. I saw them again at the house of some friends in Washington, DC. Later we all got to be very good friends. I remain in contact with Harvey and Prentiss to this day. I really enjoyed seeing all of them reunited at their Vocal Group Hall of Fame and Rock and Roll Hall of Fame inductions.

I know a lot about Otis Redding. We worked together throughout the state of Georgia and during an Irving Feld tour. At one point, Otis told me that his bus had broken down on him and he had left it in Orlando. If I wanted it I could go get it. I didn't, but maybe I should have taken him up on that offer.

I met Louie "Satchmo" Armstrong through a friend Helen Roll in New York. Her son Raymond had married Louie's niece. We would visit the family in Long Island. He was a down to earth guy who would sit on the floor and talk. We would have good visits – a great guy.

The Coasters - Carl Gardner, Bobby Nunn, Billy Guy, Dub Jones, and Cornell Gunther – were a part of the Atlantic family. Carl recently recalled when he, Dub, and Cornell backed Laverne Baker on her "Jim Dandy" recording. I knew them to be real nice guys. My group still does a few shows every year with Carl's group The Coasters, sometimes billed as The Original Coasters.

Della Reese was on a long tour with us. She was the singer for the Erskine Hawkins Band, and a good friend.

- - - - - -

It was always good to be on a package tour with a bus. Seating on artist tour buses was the other way around from what was traditional. We always sat in the front and the whites sat in the back. That way, they easily could drop us off in the Colored neighborhoods for room and board, and then go on to their lodging. When they picked us up the next day, the back of the bus was full and everybody was set. The arrangement made loading and unloading everybody and all of their baggage much easier.

I remember Eddie Cockran watching me shoot dice. I was down to my last dime. I guess "There ain't no cure for the summertime blues." He said, "Looks like you're about out of money Buddy". He reached in his pocket and gave me fifty dollars. It was a lucky fifty, because I won mine back and some more too. When I tried to return his money, he refused to take it.

Bill Haley and I became very good friends during an Irving Feld tour. Bill had an upright bass player who used to ride it like a horse. He would be playing and spanking that bass.

I crossed paths with many up and coming artists whose names are still fondly recalled today. I met The Isley Brothers when they were about 8, 9, or 10 years old.

The Drifters were traveling with The Platters, The Flamingos, and Frankie Lyman & The Teenagers. We had
a good laugh when Little Frankie fell out of the luggage
rack where he slept. Gay and Tony Williams (Platters)
were seatmates, and Zeke Carey (Flamingos) and I were
seatmates.

When we would get off the bus, Herb Reed (Platters)
would walk all over the town. He recently spoke about a
job in Memphis, where the Whites were seated upstairs
and the Blacks were seated downstairs, and somebody
through a bottle starting a big brawl. We also spoke of
how they would use different color record labels for White
and Black artists.

- - - - - -

I know Don and Phil, The Everly Brothers, well. We
worked with them when they were promoting their new
hit "Wake Up Little Susie". We were stars, and they really respected that. They were from Kentucky, but they
had moved to Nashville. They told us if we ever come to
Nashville, we would have a big picnic out on the lawn.
And I enjoyed their music.

When we played a week to ten-day gig for Clifford Miller in Memphis. We worked with some personable young guys, The Four Aims. They were just getting going good, and they could sing. We had a great time on that tour with them. They ended up having to change their group name because it sounded too much like The Ames Brothers. The name did. They didn't. They had their own style. It wasn't too long after, that they took their new name to the brand new Motown Recording Company up in Detroit, and to music stardom. Levi Stubbs, Abdul "Duke" Fakir, Renaldo "Obie" Benson, and Lawrence Payton became known to the word as The Four Tops.

Duke and I talked about those fun days when I saw him representing his group when they were inducted into the third class of the Vocal Group Hall of Fame in 2000.

- - - - - -

Jackie Wilson had left group singing and was going strong recording a string of solo hits. He told me that all he got was an apartment, some clothes, and a little spending money. He had such great talent.

- - - - - -

Some road stories stand out more than others. We were on the Rock and Roll Road Show bus together – Buddy Holly & The Crickets, The Big Bopper, Frankie Lymon & the Teenagers, The Flamingos, The Diamonds, and fifteen year old Canadian teenager Paul Anka. Another luggage rack sleeper, he recorded "Diana", written about his babysitter.

I will always remember Buddy Holly from Lubbock, Texas. We became good friends. He told me that he was working construction pushing a wheelbarrow when he found out that his record "Peggy Sue", originally "Betty Lou", was a hit.

It was so scorching hot under the late afternoon sky. We were all very hungry. And we had many miles yet to go. Buddy, self-appointed to be in charge, asked the driver to stop at the next roadside diner so we could get some food. All the Colored guys kind of looked around at each other because we knew they didn't serve Colored folks in diners in the 1950's south. We had plenty of those kinds of experiences. It was understood that we were not welcome except to perform shows.

Buddy was determined. So we all went inside together and sat down. When Buddy started to place the food orders, they told him that he would have to order out the food for the Coloreds. When they refused to serve us inside, Buddy calmly told the employees that they could eat the food. He cancelled the whole order, and everyone walked out. On that day, like on many others, Buddy and the other white Artists did what they could do to stand up for the human rights of fellow Artists.

We all rode together and became very good friends on those tour buses. I always wondered why the public couldn't do the same. Music has done more, or just as much as anything else, to help people erase racial and cultural barriers.

BUDDY HOLLY

It was a shame that I had put my life on the line for my country in the war, but I couldn't find food and rest like everyone else. We could perform almost anywhere, but we had to eat and stay only in Colored neighborhoods.

Reggie Kimber recalls:

"Bill has been like a Daddy to many for years on the road. I was the guitar player and the youngest one out there. I recall us having a sum total of $1.80. Bill stopped at a little roadside store. He went into the store and bought a loaf of bread, and some sliced bologna and cheese. We all made sandwiches and had one slice of bread, one slice of meat, and one piece of cheese left. Since I was 'the baby', Bill made me eat the other half sandwich.

"I remember at one restaurant when they found out that The Drifters were there, it seemed like the whole menu changed. A fifty cent hamburger shot right up to two dollars. Bill always got up early in the morning, doing something to make ends meet. He was up, out making contacts, going through the Black Book, making phone calls, etc. We caught hell out there sometimes, but he kept it together.

"We had an upcoming gig and we had no uniforms. We stopped at a motel / restaurant. Somehow Bill bargained for the red waiters' jackets. The people commented about how good we looked in those 'uniforms.'

"The Drifters, Bill, Gay, Bubba, and Little Dave, were in Montgomery preparing to head to the next job in Burlington, NC for Duckey Lewis. He helped book James Brown a lot in the area when 'Please, Please, Please' came out. We paid the hotel bill and loaded up.

"The car died. Bill knew the local funeral director and went to see him. There was an old hearse out back. Somehow Bill wound up with it. We loaded it up and hit the road. Bubba and I were riding in the back. He said 'I wonder how many dead bodies have been in here?' I didn't want to think about it.

"We were about a half hour late getting to Burlington. When the folks heard we had arrived, some of them came outside. To our surprise they said 'That's cool. The Drifters got a hearse.' And to think that some later rock stars actually thought THEY invented the unusual."

- - - - - -

I'm happy that I was a part of that era – coming together with nothing to fear, and making great music. Of course, none of us realized at the time how great that music was and would become, and how long it would last.

Life on the road for The Drifters had its ups and downs, but I had to keep it going. You just have to keep going in life. And I have.

CHAPTER 10
DIFFERENCES

The fellows kept complaining to me about not getting paid enough. They asked me, as their Spokesperson, to talk to the manager. I tried to talk to him about it, but he wouldn't give one bit. I was picking up the money at the gigs, and I knew he could do better by the singers.

After the meeting, he called the other guys together and told them I was fired. Not knowing any of this, I drove down to Washington, DC for our next job at the Howard Theater. I parked my car and went in the stage door. I heard them singing "I've Got To Get Myself A Woman".

As I walked backstage with my uniforms, my driver Lacy Hollingsworth met me. He said, "They got rid of you and fired Bubba too. You asked for more money and Bubba pitched a fit when he heard you were fired. He asked them 'How can you fire Bill? He IS The Drifters?'" I sat down and watched the show with Charlie Hughes and Tommy Evans in place of Bubba and me. They were way off.

- - - - -

I just went and formed a new group. I started to call it The Vigilanties, then kept the popular bird theme with The Flyers. I already had Bobby Hendricks. We got with Billy Kennedy, a guy with good booking contacts, in Eastern Shore, Maryland. "He looked like what every good singer wished he could look like", according to Bobby. D. Ernie Bailey from Baltimore rounded it out, with guitarist Reggie Kimber. We recorded "My Only Desire" / "On Bended Knee" with Bobby on lead for Herb Abramson's Atlantic subsidiary, Atco. My plan was to take this group, do more recording, and hit the road.

Before I could get it going good with The Flyers, the old manager called in early '57 and asked me to come back. Once I had returned, I found out that Johnny Moore had been drafted into the Army. Then they wanted to know if I could get Bobby Hendricks from my group to join us. I contacted him and brought him in to join me, Gay, and Charlie Hughes (Bubba's replacement). We went to work, with me as the Road Manager. I knew about the money, and the guys kept asking me about raises. I kept talking to the manager, but he got tired of it.

Since he now had a lead singer, they were ready to get rid of me again by early 1958. I told Bobby about it and asked him what he wanted to do. To his credit, he said, "It's your call". I told him to "stick with it and do a good job". Then later, Bobby quit on his own.

- - - - -

I had remarried and my son Darryl was born in 1957. Meanwhile, Clyde's solo career was going good. He married Mary Peake. Her parents owned the Carlotta Supper Club in Greensboro, North Carolina.

- - - - -

I wrote "After The Hop", a sequel to "At The Hop" by Danny and the Juniors, and "Sally's Got A Sister", a takeoff on Little Richard's "Long Tall Sally". Along with a studio group, I recorded them under the name Bill Pinkney & The Turks. Bill Justice played on that Memphis session.

But I always kept the thought in the back of my mind about my sacrifices for and my contributions to The Drifters.

BOBBY HOLLIS, GERHARDT THRASHER,
ANDREW THRASHER, AND BILL PINKNEY

CHAPTER 11
THE ORIGINAL DRIFTERS

There was real trouble brewing. The manager decided to get rid of the guys that were left and use another group under The Drifters' name for an upcoming Apollo engagement. He said he could replace them and they were all fired. He said The Drifters were his and there was nothing anybody could do about it.

When I heard about it, I didn't agree. You see, none of the original members had signed any management agreements with him. I had recruited every one of the lead singers, and I had given years of blood, sweat, and tears to keep my promise to Clyde to keep the group going. I had gotten the jobs done to please the public.

Although I didn't know about the legal side of the business, I sure knew plenty about the performing side. I felt like I was entitled to some consideration.

Meanwhile, I formed Bill Pinkney and the Originals. I contacted Gay, Bubba, and Little Dave. Except for Clyde's absence, it was the closest thing to getting the Original Drifters back together. We created magic once, and we were going to go for it again.

We recorded "Gee" and "Santa Clause is Coming to Town" on the End record label using the name The Harmony Grits, but the ad in Billboard had the sub-caption "formerly the Original Drifters". We kept on doing our same Drifters show that WE were known for.

- - - - - -

A card carrying union member, I sought relief through arbitration in the American Guild of Variety Artists (AGVA). Mr. Bunn, who was in charge, scheduled an arbitration hearing and Delores Rosario presided. The old manager was there with his lawyer and two new singers. I had my manager Esther Navarro and the "Originals" with me.

My case was plain and simple. I didn't think it was right that the one who was there from the beginning, who had kept it alive, who had recruited every significant member, and who had dealt with all that comes with being on the road could just be tossed aside like old clothes. None of the original members had ever signed management agreements or contracts with the so-called manager. I talked about my contributions to The Drifters' name and our success. I wanted the name "Original Drifters".

When their lawyer responded, I didn't understand some of the legal talk. But I did know that I was an American and a union member that should have some rights that I had to protect.

After some more discussion, it was decision time. AGVA agreed with me and I prevailed. I was given the "exclusive and irrevocable" name / mark "Original Drifters". Bill Pinkney & The Originals became "Bill Pinkney & The Original Drifters" that day, committed to keeping alive the sounds of the fifties.

- - - - - -

Esther Navarro started booking us through Universal Attractions in New York. Ben Bart was in charge and we had a good business relationship. We kept touring, just as we had been doing, except now we booked under my name "Original Drifters". I have used "Original Drifters" in some form usually with my own name since then.

- - - - - -

February of 1959 was a very sad time for the music industry and the fans. A fatal airplane crash took the life of Buddy Holly, along with Ritchie Valens and The Big Bopper. I think the trauma of that accident is a lot of the reason why many of the Artists even today will not fly on propeller airplanes.

But we keep going.

MY DAUGHTER EARTHA'S 7TH BIRTHDAY

CHAPTER 12
THE DECADE OF THE 1960'S

As the decade of the sixties rolled in, two groups of Drifters were on the move. We were out on the road, and the new guys were recording and releasing good songs. They needed new songs to help identify them. Their voices on our songs weren't working well with the public that already knew the originals and our voices.

I always thought it was interesting how Atlantic kept the buying public confused by releasing records with us on one side and the others on the flip side.

"Honey Bee" / "Some Kind of Wonderful"
"Suddenly There's A Valley" / "I Count The Tears"
"No Sweet Lovin'" / "Please Stay"

Each group had to sing the other's songs, because folks bought both of them on one record. When they came to a show, they expected all of them. They had that right.

But that personnel revolving door kept going like in the 50's because of bad management wanting to own the entertainers, to not pay them decently, and to control their minds. They didn't understand or didn't want to understand the mind of an independent artist. So they would use a guy just long enough to record him a lot and then replace him.

Ben E. King is a good example. He left after a shorter stay than most people realize. He said he wrote "Stand By Me" for The Drifters, but it was rejected. Bennie made it a smash solo hit. His manager, Lover Patterson, sent Bennie and me with two other singers to do a Drifters job together in Ohio. I can still remember that trip in Lover's '58 Olds.

Chuck Jackson shared his thoughts on the time:

> "I traveled a lot with Clyde in the '60's, and he became my neighbor in Teanek, NJ. I hadn't met Bill, but I knew of him. He has become one of my favorite people.

"I was about 12 or 13 still in South Carolina when 'White Christmas' came out. I had an after school job cleaning a three room office suite for attorney Norwood Gasque. I sat behind his desk with my feet up on it one day and hit some buttons on his Dictaphone. 'White Christmas' came on the radio. I sat there and tried to sing Bill's bass, and, since I still had a light voice then, I tried to sing Clyde's tenor. But I heard Mr. Gasque coming, so I hurried back to work. Imagine my surprise when he later gave me the tape from his dictaphone. He said 'You are going to be a great singer some day'. I thought to myself 'If I could record then, I could do it again.' I will always have a special fondness for The Drifters, because that was my start."

Bobby Hollis recalls the period this way:

"Bill Pinkney came to Long Island, NY to get me to audition. Thank God he picked me, because it gave me an opportunity to learn a lot about life and motivated me to do some exciting things. I left New York in my green Chevy and went down South. Bill kept us working. People would come to him and deal direct because he definitely had the best performing group. A lot of artists are great studio artists, but not the best performers. When Bill put a combo together, they knew what they were doing.

"Our first trip to Japan was out of Dallas. When we came back, we went on a college tour. We would work from Thursday through Sunday all over the place. We were back in Dallas when Rev. Dr. Martin Luther King, Jr. was assassinated. We left that Wednesday night for a show in Augusta, GA on Thursday. The show was cancelled.

"We recorded 'Do The Jerk' and 'Don't Call Me, I'll Call You' in Los Angeles for Fontana Records. Jimmy Lewis, a great showman, wrote the last one. While we were in Dallas, we recorded 'Tumbleweed'. I recall Kenneth Falkner and Tom Bullock, a motorcycle cop, well. Jimmy Velvit drove up in a red Chevy and helped us when the bus broke down. We didn't encounter much racism in the 60's. We were always welcome wherever we went. I have some great memories of Clyde McPhatter's three or four month 'Hot Five' tour with many R&B Legends of today.

"I nicknamed Bill 'Wool'. He is like good material. It will hold up a long time. He has been a provider for a lot of people and has helped a lot of people over the years."

Clyde McPhatter 's Hot Five Tour in the mid '60's, featured Clyde, The Original Drifters, and rotating acts - Jimmy Reed, Aaron Neville, Joe Tex (in a new '64 Cadillac), Bo Diddley, Otis Redding, and James and Bobby Purifoy from Pensacola.

Dick Allen from Universal Attractions was the road manager and Jimmy Oliver was the bandleader. In fact, Jimmy wrote "Ta Ta" for Clyde. The tour ran for about four months moving throughout the south stopping in Georgia, Oklahoma, Missouri, Alabama, Arkansas, and Texas. The public received us well – hearing the real recording artists singing their songs.

Clyde's distant cousin Rudy McPhatter recalled talking with Clyde about career turns:

"Clyde told me that he didn't like the deal he got stuck with after the service. He never forgave himself for not coming back to the group because he really was a quartet singer. He got talked into going solo, and he said he always regretted it.

He said that his manager, who wasn't really the group's manager, talked him into it."

Esther Navarro was still managing Bill Pinkney & The Original Drifters. She and her partner Irv Nahan got us a job at a Louisiana club. We took the long drive down there to do the gig. When we walked in the door, they were completely shocked when they saw us. Why? They said they didn't know they had been listening to Colored folks on their records, and they definitely did not want us to perform in their club. Then they gave us five hundred dollars, and told us we could leave. Of course, we took the money and left. I wonder if they bought any more Drifters records?

But it wasn't like that everywhere in the South. I guess the folks in Dallas knew what to expect when we came, for we had a great gig with Roy Orbison at The Guthrie.

- - - - - -

When I was living at the Sir John Hotel in Miami, I went to the same barbershop with Sam Moore, maybe just hitting twenty. He was working local with his partner Dave Prater. They opened for us when we had a run at the King of Hearts Club in Miami for Johnny Lomella.

Sam and Dave went on to have some smash hits with the "Memphis sound". Who can forget "Soul Man" and "When Something is Wrong With My Baby"?

While working in that area, I had the chance to meet and make friends with many baseball players during their spring training. Some were Jackie Robinson and Roy Campanella (Brooklyn Dodgers), Satchel Paige, Larry Doby, and Luke Easter (Cleveland Indians), Elston Howard (New York Yankees), Willie Mays and Hank Thompson (New York Giants), and Buck O'Neal.

- - - - - -

Chuck Berry and I go back a long way to the sixties when we first worked together in Dallas. When we worked together in Atlanta in 2001, he made people put their cameras down – no photos or videos.

We often had well known people in our audiences many places we went. I recall when we worked in Los Angeles for Mr. Sullivan, both Muhammad Ali and Stevie Wonder came to our show. This was just after Ali had won at the Olympics, and shortly before he changed his name from Cassius Clay. I always admired the way he stood up for what he believed in and commanded respect for it.

I was pleased to see the other Drifters following in our footsteps and helping to carry on the legacy that was started in 1953. They added another dimension to a well established name, and I was proud of them for their own success. And I truly treasure the friendships and mutual respect that last to this day.

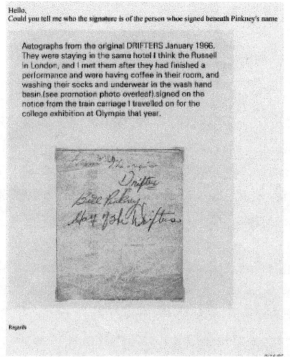

Hello,
Could you tell me who the signature is of the person whose signed beneath Pinkney's name

Autographs from the original DRIFTERS January 1966. They were staying in the same hotel I think the Russell in London, and I met them after they had finished a performance and were having coffee in their room, and washing their socks and underwear in the wash hand basin.(see promotion photo overleaf).signed on the notice from the train carriage I travelled on for the college exhibition at Olympia that year.

Regards

AUTOGRAPHS OF BILL AND GERHARDT IN 1966
LONDON, ENGLAND

In the mid 60's, the mainstream market demand for rhythm and blues went down when the "British invasion" hit. So we reversed it. Bill Pinkney & The Original Drifters kept rolling, going to England in January of 1966 for a college exhibition tour for British promoter Roy Tempest. We alternated venues with Patti LaBelle & The Bluebells, starting at Olympia. The reception there was great. We stayed at the Russell Hotel in London. When that tour was over, we returned to home to a slower market in general, but we kept working.

FROM LEFT TO RIGHT: GERHARDT THRASHER, BOBBY HENDRICKS, BOBBY HOLLIS, AND BILL PINKNEY

Harry Turner wrote:

"But a particular performance by The Drifters one night blew me away totally. The group was in the middle of the Joe Tex hit 'Hold What You Got' when suddenly the lead singer collapsed on stage. We were thunderstruck, as all efforts to revive him failed. The other Drifters picked him up, and carried him offstage to the dressing room, while we sat in stunned silence. Strangely enough, the band continued to play softly in the background when, all of a sudden, we heard this blood curdling scream. The 'stricken' Drifter was running towards us, with the other Drifters in hot pursuit. He leaped onto the stage, landed on his knees, slid across the stage as he grabbed the mike, and continued singing in tempo with the music as the rest of the group joined him to finish the song.

"We gave them a rousing, though relieved, standing ovation. The whole thing had been totally staged and choreographed, and we fell for it all the way. It may have been hokey, but they pulled it off with total precision and drama."

- - - - - -

The former manager died in 1967. I am told that his widow moved to England in the early 1970's and formed a group around Johnny Moore. I have heard that they had some success abroad until Johnny passed away in December of 1998.

- - - - - -

When we were in motels along the way, I never missed a chance to watch baseball on television. I recall the special pride I felt when my hometown friend Bobby Richardson hit the home run that won the World Series for the New York Yankees. I wasn't necessarily a Yankees fan, but I sure was a Bobby Richardson fan.

The road got rough at times. We were parked for three days near a Lakeland, Florida orange grove. We didn't have any money or food, but we had plenty of oranges. I guess you know what we ate.

- - - - - -

Bill Griffin owned, the biggest club in Greensboro, North Carolina, The Castaways. He got many jobs for us over the years. Cecil Corbitt, his friend, was one of the area's biggest promoters. Years later, Cecil was the one who inducted me into the Beach Music Hall of Fame.

Maurice Williams, well known for his hit "Stay" recalls:

"I remember meeting Bill through my manager Harry Goings. It was a great pleasure. We hit it off so well and we were from the same state. He was a wonderful person and a go-getter. We became like family and shared thoughts together. I had no idea he had sung that great bass lead on 'White Christmas'.

"They were filming a part of the *Dirty Dancing* movie at Lake Lewell, NC. Eleanor Burnstein, who wrote the movie, presented me with a Platinum Album for 'Stay' from that movie. I will never forget when we did the *Dirty Dancing Show* then with The Ink Spots and The Original Drifters. Some white dancers came out on stage and sang 'Stay'. Bill said 'What are they doing? That's your song, you're the Originator.' It is a beautiful memory that he spoke in protection of a little brother and didn't want anybody stepping on me."

- - - - - -

We had many positive times in the fifties and sixties. Besides all of the wonderful Atlantic artists, we had the pleasure of working with many other great entertainers as we toured – Ella Fitzgerald at the Howard Theater, Dakota Staton, Pearl Bailey, Peggy Lee, Billy Eckstine, Peg Leg Bates, and Nat "King" Cole. And we worked with many, many singing groups.

I certainly must mention the great road bands of Erskine Hawkins, Benny Green, Red Prysock, Rusty Bryant, and Sil Austin.

ANTOINE "FATS" DOMINO

THE PLATTERS

SONNY TIL & THE ORIOLES

THE CHARMS

RUTH BROWN

LEE ANDREWS
AND THE HEARTS

THE COASTERS

HANK BALLARD

THE FIESTAS

THE HEARTBEATS

LAVERNE BAKER

LITTLE ANTHONY
& THE IMPERIALS

THE EL DORADOS

CHUCK JACKSON

THE FIVE ROYALES

THE HARPTONES

THE SOLITAIRES

DELLA REESE

THE DELLS

THE FIVE SATINS

DAKOTA STATON

THE FALCONS

THE PENGUINS   THE CLOVERS

THE FIVE KEYS   THE RAVENS

THE MOONGLOWS

THE INK SPOTS

THE FLAMINGOS

CHAPTER 13
THE DECADE OF THE 1970'S

We had survived the so-called "British Invasion" of the sixties. Some of those very artists had cited us and other rhythm and blues artists as their early influences.

Now the country was going disco. Everybody seemed to be dancing and jumping. But there still was a market for the music of the fifties. I just had to keep finding it to keep The Original Drifters name going.

Helen Greer-Gordon recalls:

"I met Bill Pinkney when my brother P.O. 'Pat' Patton was Bill's bus driver in the early 1970's. I was a music promoter in Atlanta. The Original Drifters were in the rotation of performers that included Chuck Jackson, Jackie Wilson, and others at the very popular Scarlet O'Hara's Night Club in Underground Atlanta.

"Pat told me that Bill was looking for a musician. I introduced him to Ali Woodson, a nineteen or twenty-year-old singer who had left a regional act and was in Atlanta working solo. Bill added Ali to his group as a musician right away and took him out on the road with the group on Ali's first trip to Vegas. Ali eventually went to the front vocal line. I later booked the group in Memphis in a beautiful place down on the waterfront.

"I have had the pleasure of working with Bill on other occasions over the years. Since relocating to Las Vegas, I have seen his fine group performance many times in the 1990's. I have always known Bill to be a gentleman who treated women in the business with great respect."

- - - - -

I was working in North Carolina when I heard the news that Clyde McPhatter had passed away in June of 1972. I called Nick Allen, a very good friend of his who grew up with him in Durham in the 30's. He confirmed the news.

CLYDE MCPHATTER

The funeral was two days later and I just couldn't get there on such short notice, because I was working. I was deeply saddened to hear that not many of his friends were there. He had set the standard for a host of great tenors who followed his lead. He deserved a full church. Clyde was buried in George Washington Memorial Park in Paramus, New Jersey, near where he lived.

I will always cherish the memory of Clyde McPhatter, the young, personable, happy go lucky kid who had such an impact on my life.

I am often asked during interviews why the music of the fifties and sixties is in demand, and what made The Drifters so special. I think the music lasts because it has a positive message about life and love. The key is that we had good writers that came up with good material. When you add that to great singers and performers, you have something that can last, and each generation plays it for the next one. I was always pleased to see young people in audiences then - and especially today.

I sing from my heart. I try to feel the people and give them what they want. To feel the soul.

- - - - -

Art Engler with Associated Booking Company was the first one to send us to Las Vegas. It was in the 1970's. We performed at the Sahara Hotel with Della Reese.

- - - - -

A "lingering dream" of Harry Turner's had been to bring a concert to upstate South Carolina. With promoter Rick Harp, he planned a real community event to benefit the American Cancer Society in April.

In his book "This Magic Moment" he reflected:

"But much like Richard Nader, I was admonished by the wagging tongues and naysayers that nobody cared about America's golden music any more. I saw a long overdue homecoming as the Drifters saw the Diamonds who greeted the Coasters, who welcomed the Clovers, who hugged Joe Bennett and the Sparkletones and on an on." Bill Pinkney and the Original Drifters were the final act of the evening. Having both emceed and viewed Bill's and Drifters' act on numerous occasions, I can unequivocally say that I have never seen them perform better than on that night. It was magical.

"Bill's salute to cofounder Clyde McPhatter charged the crowd with an emotion as he offered, in his unique bass-baritone voice, Clyde's hit 'Without Love'. The group was so on-the-mark that even the other entertainers gathered around just off stage in the wings to watch their performance. From halfway through the Drifters' set until they left the stage, the entire house was standing. Remaining on their feet, the whole crowd roared their fervent approval as the Drifters closed their set. MORE!' 'MORE!' 'MORE' 'MORE!' they chanted as they refused to let the Drifters leave the stage. I was right there chanting 'MORE' along with them.

"When all of the artists returned for the finale, 'concert-goers were actually hysterical, some standing in their seats. Many others were dancing in the aisles, jumping up and down, and yelling and singing along, while the various entertainers took turns singing the lead and answering each other in the best gospel call – and - shout tradition. There was more love in the air than at a gospel revival. It was the same for me as it had been for Richard Nader and Dick Clark in Madison Square Garden a few years earlier.

"The once dubious auditorium manager rushed over, and gushed that the show was the greatest program he had ever been associated with, and that the talent we had all witnessed was beyond anything imaginable.

"Strangely, America's golden music is overtly more popular, more appreciated, and more revered overseas than in the U.S. The late Marv Johnson…told me that on (a) European tour with

The Temptations he was continually overwhelmed by the fans' enthusiasm, knowledge of the music and deep love for its pioneers.

"America's golden music is uniquely American and must be claimed as a part of our rich cultural history. It is as timeless as our souls. Its lyrics speak to us and its beat carries us, lifting our spirits, enriching our lives and the lives of future generations. In a troubled world, this incredible music, thanks to its creators, has the power to bring us closer together, crossing boundaries that separate and divide."

- - - - - -

We had just finished performing and had some time off. Since I was in my own car, I told the other fellows go on ahead to their homes and I would catch up with them later before the next gig.

I had been on the road a lot, and I was just close enough to stop through home and surprise my Mother. It was Sunday morning. She was in the kitchen cooking when I got there. She was so glad to see me. We sat down in the living room and we were having a wonderful talk.

And then she just slumped right over out of her chair onto the floor. I picked her up, ran out to my car with her, and rushed her straight to the hospital. But by the time I got her there, she was gone.

I called Gay to notify him and have him let the group know about my Mama. His wife answered the phone. Before I asked to speak with Gay, I told his wife.

She stopped me and said, "I was just getting ready to try and get in touch with you. Gay passed."

- - - - - -

We kept going. We kept working.

CHAPTER 14
UNTITLED

My friend Brook Benton came to South Carolina to visit
The Williams family, his cousins. It was a great reunion
for us too. A reporter did an interview with us for the area
newspaper talking about our careers in music. Brook
said, "Fame is a name, but success is something inward
– something that happens inside you.

BROOK BENTON, FRANK WILLIAMS, SR., AND BILL

- - - - - -

Marshak called asking to meet with me in 1981. He said that he was promoting shows with my cousin Dock Green, Elsbeary Hobbs, and Charlie Thomas as The Drifters.

I agreed to meet with him. We met and we discussed his proposal.

He said that the singers applied for The Drifters' name and that they assigned the mark to him. He wanted a written agreement to outline the differences in the two groups of touring Drifters, while acknowledging and pro-tecting my ongoing use of The Original Drifters mark. We made that agreement.

He went his way and I went mine. At least for a while.

- - - - - -

Although he had made no contribution to the legacy, one of my former singers had decided to form a group of his own and call it The Original Drifters.

Promoter Tommie Price was there:

"I went down with Bill in about 1981 to Charleston, SC Federal Court on Broad and Meeting Streets. Bobby Peoples was driving a new car and took us there. Harold Thomas was managing and promoting a group calling themselves 'The Original Drifters', and we went down for the hearing. A lawyer came down from New Jersey. Thomas & Co. lost that case. I remember the front page of the Charleston News and Courier the next day. There was a picture of a singer Benny Anderson coming out of the Court House with his head down. I saved that newspaper for a long time.

"The Court proved that a singer who joins a name group after its legacy is established cannot claim credit for what went on before he came along and go out and use the name when separating from that group.

"I had the privilege of promoting or assisting with many Original Drifters engagements in the 80's. There was a big concert in Jackson, Tennessee, three weeks at Captain Bilbrow's, a floating restaurant on the pier in Memphis, and a lot of things at Boondock's in North Carolina. That place looked like a haunted house back in the field. They worked also for the 25th Anniversary of the Eastland Mall in Detroit in 1984."

- - - - - -

I crossed paths occasionally with The Dixie Humming-birds of Philly and The Swanee Quintet from August, Georgia. They were old friends. I had the pleasure of meeting them in the 50's. Their groups were like broth-ers to The Drifters.

CHAPTER 15
ROCK AND ROLL HALL OF FAME

As I stood on stage thirty-five years after The Drifters' founding being inducted into the Rock and Roll Hall of Fame, I was thrilled and I was proud. The Drifters, The Supremes, The Beach Boys, The Beatles, Les Paul, and Bob Dylan were all inducted on January 20, 1988. A real emotional highlight of the evening came when The Supremes' Mary Wilson spoke lovingly of her fellow group singer, the Late Florence Ballard, with Florence's daughters at her side.

They recognized the seven significant contributors to The Drifters legacy – organizer Clyde McPhatter, and Gerhardt Thrasher and myself, as original members, and later members Johnny Moore, Benjamin Nelson (Ben E. King), Charlie Thomas, and Rudy Lewis.

Ahmet Ertegun spoke of the beginning. He went to the Birdland Lounge to see Billy Ward & The Dominoes because he enjoyed lead Clyde McPhatter and wanted to hear him sing. No Clyde. After the show, Billy told Ahmet that Clyde had been fired. So Ahmet checked the phone book and found three McPhatters listed. Clyde's father answered on the first call. Soon Clyde's unmistakable voice was on the phone. And, as they say, the rest is history. Ahmet himself had proclaimed The Drifters as the "all time greatest Atlantic group".

ROCK AND ROLL HALL OF FAME SIGNATURE WALL

After singer Billy Joel had spoken with great respect about how The Drifters music had encouraged him and his young gang member friends to reach for the sky, he welcomed Clyde's widow, Johnny, Benny, Charlie, and me to the stage for official induction. They all stepped back and Charlie Thomas said, "Bill, you speak first, because you're the oldest".

"Well, I guess all of the guys, these kids, they want me to go first because I'm their father. They call me the Father of The Drifters because I was along with Clyde McPhatter in 1953 right here in New York City where we first got started with the Atlantic Records. Believe it or not, it was a long hard struggle. But it was a great struggle.

"It brought us here after thirty five years to the Rock and Roll Hall of Fame. And it didn't only do that. It also kept The Drifters in touch with one another. Even though we are not together all the time in person, in our hearts and our minds we are together. And tonight, Johnny, Charlie, Benny, and Mrs. McPhatter, it's a pleasure."

I appreciated the recognition and respect in Johnny's remarks. "I want to thank first Clyde McPhatter who started the group. I want to thank Bill Pinkney who gave me the chance to come into The Drifters by calling the manager and telling him '…I've got a guy and I think he can do it'. I watched Bill keep The Drifters alive". I thought back to 1954 when I overheard him singing in the men's room in Cleveland.

And I recall Charlie telling of how he sneaked into the side door of the Apollo Theater to see The Drifters, even though he was an under-aged sixteen years old. He still laughs about it today. Charlie came to me when they were first hired as The Drifters. He said, "Bill, I'm sorry about what happened. We are still friends. No matter what, I love you Man, and we'll always be friends. You are the Original." And we're still friends today.

Benny was excited. He expressed his appreciation to the founders with great respect. And everyone really enjoyed Lena McPhatter's remarks closing with "I don't sing, but I feel like I'm a "Drifter"".

I was thrilled to share the stage and receive the same professional credit with all of my great fellow entertainers at New York Waldorf-Astoria Hotel in a room filled with people who understood and appreciated what we all had worked so hard over the years to achieve.

We had a serious jam session that night!

MY ROCK AND ROLL HALL OF FAME TROPHY

- - - - - -

A short time before The Drifters' Rock and Roll Hall of
Fame induction, Andrew (Bubba) Thrasher passed away.
He had been sick and was in the hospital for some time.
Johnny Moore and I went to the funeral.

Since that day in 1988, I have been the only living member of the group of men who formed The Drifters.

CHAPTER 16
VIVA LAS VEGAS

About six weeks after the Rock and Roll Hall of Fame induction, The Original Drifters opened a two-week engagement in Las Vegas. It's an exciting town, bright lights, great sights, good food, and wonderful people. I suppose all artists want to play Vegas, and we loved it.

The Four Queens French Quarter Lounge, downtown on world famous Fremont Street, was the premiere 50's and 60's music venue. It drew locals and tourists alike. We got great revues and drew sellout crowds. We received an offer for an extended contract for multiple dates of two to four weeks at a time.

I had the pleasure of meeting and visiting with Herbert Mills of The Mills Brothers. He greeted me with "Hey there, young fellow". So many of my fellow artists and friends passed through Vegas and stopped to say hello – The Shirelles, The Platters, The Diamonds, The Coasters, The Flamingos, Gary U.S. Bonds, The Temptations, Joe Williams, Greg Morris, Arthur and Red Prysock, Danny and the Juniors, Jewel Aikens, Rudy Ray Moore, Redd Foxx, and many more. Most of them would join us on stage. Of course, the audiences loved that. After all, we are there to please the public.

- - - - - -

I met Maxine in Vegas when I came off the stage one night in 1988. She said it was great to see me still touring since the first time she met me. Met me? She recalled walking past Underground Atlanta's Scarlet O'Hara's in 1972 and hearing The Original Drifters performing. She came in and we spoke briefly after the show. She said that the name Pinkney was in her family tree and she had South Carolina roots too. Although I didn't have any reason to remember this brief conversation, the name stuck with her. When she saw the name in the Las Vegas newspaper, she came to see our show. We became well acquainted by telephone over the next few months. By the time I got back to work in Vegas, I felt that this independent businesswoman would become a very dear friend. And I had four weeks to work on it.

- - - - -

I was during this engagement that I got the news that Brook Benton had passed away. The news was a real blow because we had been great friends for so long. Since he was a first cousin to my South Carolina friends, the Williams family – sisters' children, we saw each other whenever we could over the years when he visited them.

Brook had come to see me earlier and he told me that he was Saved. I remember his words, "You just don't know how beautiful it will be when you go home to meet the Lord. I know I'm sick, but I'm happy."

The family asked me to speak at his Homegoing service. I made arrangements to fly back from Vegas to honor that request at the service at Trinity United Methodist Church in Camden, South Carolina and the burial at his home church, Ephesus United Methodist Church, in Lugoff, South Carolina.

Brook made such beautiful music. I sometimes sing "Rainy Night in Georgia", "Kiddies", or "It's Just a Matter Of Time" in my shows even now as a tribute to him.

- - - - - -

Everyone lovingly called Maxine's mother "Dr. Mom". She was the perfect person to sit down and talk to. One of the most genuine, kind, and wonderful women I have ever met, we hit it off well.

So did Maxine and I. She joined me six weeks later in Atlantic City when we played the Atlantis Casino. A bad snowstorm grounded flights, so the planned four-day trip turned into a week. In fact, she ended up having to take a bus from Atlantic City to Newark to get a flight back home to Vegas.

On my off night, we caught a show by my friend Nipsey Russell at Harrah's. Long ago, Nipsey had given me some good advice on how to double my money – fold it and put it back in my pocket!

CHAPTER 17
TROUBLE IN THE AIR

I had no idea what was about to happen a couple of days later. That's when I learned a hard and costly lesson. The bitter truth is that every artist must have knowledge-able entertainment counsel. The simple agreement with Marshak was not so simple after all.

Marshak surfaced as the plaintiff in a legal action against the casino and me claiming that we had infringed on his mark. The ads read "The Drifters" instead of "The Original Drifters". He had given no opportunity for correction. He was not willing to hear anything about an honest mistake.

I had worked for two weeks and had to pay my guys, but the money was held up with legal maneuvering pending a court decision. During the course of things, I could see that this would be a long drawn out situation.

One of my acquaintances intercepted "strategy letters" outlining plans to run me out of business through the expense of multiple lawsuits against me. Before long suits started popping up other places. Some didn't have much substance, but they were expensive to defend just like the letters predicted. It took years, then more years on appeal, before the funds were released – and then paying only some of the legal fees.

But I kept doing my thing, and I let the lawyers do theirs. I had to keep it going.

CHAPTER 18
ABOUT MONEY AND RESPECT

While I was on a Vegas job, I spoke with Ruth Brown by telephone. She gave me an earful about her ongoing efforts to get Atlantic, and the industry as a whole, to give accurate sales accountings, to pay fair royalties to artists, and to make proper union reports.

She described the problem this way in her book:

"Atlantic had converted all their old acts to their new computer system, mixing in old and new artists willy-nilly regardless of the enormous differentials in royalty rates. Unlike our old five percent top, current artists' rates, … twelve to fifteen percent and up, had been negotiated to stand current practices, such as getting paid only half-rate on foreign earnings, treating ten percent of sales as 'free goods'; charging twelve percent for packaging, bearing the costs of 'remastering, remixing, and editing'. Right away, a minimum of twenty five percent of sales was being discounted and thrown right out the window.

"How did Atlantic justify lumping their old artists in with this? Oh, it was impossible to keep two systems running ...so it had to be...the *new* way. The sales of the older stars, their rationale ran, were not significant enough to justify the setting-up of a separate system. So whether by accident or design they had set things up to pay less than what they should. (Attorney) Howell (Beagle) ... sum(med) it up this way: 'They've been stacking all the charges of a *modern* contract against an *ancient* five percent royalty."

It came to a head in April, 1988, as reported by Richard Harrington under the *Washington Post* newspaper headline

ATLANTIC'S BOW TO THE BLUES HERITAGE:
Label Is Recalculating
Royalty Payments and Committing
$1.5 Million to Rhythm and Blues Foundation."

Again, my telephone calls to Atlantic went nowhere. I couldn't even talk to them about my overdue money. Finally, Ruth referred me to Chuck Rubin. With his assurance that he would get my money, I got him through his Artists Rights Enforcement to contact them.

It seems strange to me that they responded to him, while not responding to me. I never understood why they would pay me through him but not pay me directly. The downside was I had to give Chuck half of the money. I did not know that he would continue to collect half of my royalty money because they would keep paying me through him. I have always felt that I was and am being ripped off by this process, just like I have been ripped off since the 1950's.

- - - - -

May of 1988 was Atlantic Record's 40th anniversary. Everyone knew about their big plans to invite their top artists over the years for the celebration. I waited and waited for the invitation that never arrived. I heard that there was a legal challenge about name use issues, so Atlantic decided to celebrate with no Drifters at all rather than use generics or face threatened litigation. I have always felt that it was a major slight.

As industry insiders and outsiders expressed disbelief, I thought back to Ahmet's positive words just a few months earlier at the Rock and Roll Hall of Fame induction. We worked very hard in those early years at Atlantic and we helped to put them on the map in a big way. Atlantic made enough money on us over the years to litigate if necessary. I believe they should have stood by the four living Hall of Fame Drifters.

Here's how Harry Turner described his anticipation:

> "I would finally get to see a true salute to the Atlantic pioneers from the 40's, 50's and 60's who made such incredible music. There would be live performances of my favorites, plus film clips and video tape of deceased artists like Clyde McPhatter, Chuck Willis, Bobby Darin, Joe Turner, Otis Redding and Ivory Joe Hunter. Also, I envisioned a backup band featuring some of the original studio musicians from the heyday of their recordings.

> "My excitement quickly soured. Original artists such as Ruth Brown, Lavern Baker, Carla Thomas, Sam Moore of Sam and Dave, and Rufus Thomas all appeared – briefly and token at best.

There was a short salute only to Otis Redding and Bobby Darin.

"My hopes were not totally dashed because there was an announcement about a powerhouse re-union of one of the all-time great singing groups yet to come. I knew it would be the Drifters, the Coasters, or the Clovers, all of whose members had separated. 'Stay tuned!' Finally 'supergroup' reunion time had arrived. In his best grandstand-ing fashion, the announcer introduced this earthshaking group. It turned out to be…not the Drifters…not the Coasters…not the Clovers…but that legendary 'pioneering' group…Led Zeppe-lin!

"Led Zeppelin? While I had no problem with a Led Zeppelin reunion being a part of the special, I was floored by that selection as the touted 'su-pergroup', especially with no invitation to Bill Pinkney and any other Drifters. Secondly, four recording members of the Coasters—Carl Gardner, Cornell Gunther, Billy Guy, and 'Dub' Jones—together for the first time in over twenty-five years, backstage. The one song The Coast-ers sang was not even one of their biggest hits.

This show illustrated the industry's lack of respect for its own roots – those forerunning, pacesetting artists who literally created the industry. In a profound display of skewed vision, the producers, and Atlantic … opted to largely ignore the true, groundbreaking pioneers."

Maxine Porter recalls.:

"The Original Drifters were on tour in Omaha, St. Louis, Kansas City, and Denver for promoter Joe Gehl performing for firefighter and police benefits. I met Dee Clark, riding on Bill's tour bus, and The Dixie Cups' Barbara and Rosa Hawkins. This was a pivotal trip, giving me a real in depth view of Bill Pinkney - the man.

"Dee, a multiple stroke survivor, didn't have much of his singing voice left and wasn't walking well. Near the end of each show, Bill would announce that there was a Special Guest in the house and bring Dee on stage to sing his big hit 'Raindrops.' Bill and Dee did it together with Bill singing the high parts that Dee couldn't hit. It always brought the house down. More importantly, it allowed Dee the dignity of earning his way while, as Bill said, 'helping me school these young guys'."

CHAPTER 19
THE EARLY 1990'S

I brought in the 1990's in Las Vegas. Since we didn't want to be traveling on Christmas day going to open at the Four Queens on the twenty sixth of December, we arrived a day early and spent Christmas there. Dr. Mom and Maxine had prepared our holiday dinner and made everyone feel like family. Later in the evening, we set up the keyboard by the fireplace in the living room for some rehearsing. We sang R&B, gospel, and holiday songs for hours. It was a wonderful Christmas to remember - filled with warmth and fellowship.

I was surprised two evenings later to be the Guest of Honor at a special reception co-hosted by Maxine and MaryLouise (Jap) Williams. It seemed that everyone knew about it but me. The hotel management recognized me as the only artist on their entertainment roster to have achieved Rock and Roll Hall of Fame induction. Many friends and colleagues turned out for it. Ed Fasulo, General Manager, offered warm words and presented me with a plaque.

There was a special air that New Years Eve. After the first show, Maxine and I went to a party hosted by her friends Dr. Andres Costas and his wife attorney/journalist Barbara Robinson. I was pleased to see my old friend Rev. O. C. Smith there. We left in time to get back for my last show. We welcomed the 1990's with a bang.

We played at Sea Word in San Antonio, Texas for the Memorial Day weekend with The Platters, Paul Revere and the Raiders, and Johnny Rivers. They drove us around in a cart for a private tour. We enjoyed seeing the dolphins, and we had the special privilege to see Shamu and have a private visit with the keeper.

In July, we spent a week at the Holiday Inn Woodlawn in Charlotte and went on to Morristown, Tennessee. Bill and Linda Bailey, Calvin and Aggie McKinney, and Ron and Peg Jordan made us feel like family and set up a real spread. Later, the Mayor gave me a key to the city.

Our next stop was Beckley, West Virginia for promoter Bill Heaberlin to play at the state amphitheater with Sha

Na Na. We made it to about the fourth song, and the sound system failed. I just stepped to the front of the stage, quieted the audience, told a couple of jokes, gave a little soft shoe, beckoned the other fellows out front, and gave the folks an *a capella* "Old Man River". When they got the sound back on, and we did a few more numbers and closed. By the time Sha Na Na came on, the clouds let forth a downpour. When we see them on the road now, we still have a chuckle about that show. Maxine still recalls that fun tour with the old-fashioned family style barbeque, the sound blackout, and running down the hill piling into a vehicle to escape the storm.

- - - - -

Every where I went, somebody mentioned it. It seemed the whole country was buzzing about the new movie "Home Alone", with my "White Christmas" right there on the soundtrack. I was pleased to learn that it was included in such a big hit movie. I just knew it was big royalty time. More than ten years later, I'm still waiting.

- - - - - -

We performed in April of 1991 on TNN's Nashville Now television show. It was a great experience even though this country music station aired it opposite the Country

Music Awards Show. We sang "Money Honey" from the 50's, "Please Stay" from the 60's, and a new song -"That Same Old Candle Light", presenting a Drifters overview. The host Ralph Emery surprised me, asking us to sing "White Christmas." Of course, we sat right there and obliged him - impromptu *a capella*.

- - - - -

In June of 1992, Dr. Mom suffered a serious stroke and Maxine became the caregiver. I remember my words to her, "Your place is with your Mother. I'm a Man, and I'll see to it that she doesn't want for anything, and you won't either." I have never seen anybody do like she did for her Mother, and I'm proud of her.

Since it put a stop to Maxine's frequent road trips, she assumed more management duties for The Original Drifters by communicating with the participating booking agencies, enhancing publicity and promotion, sorting out legal issues, and developing an internet presence.

And we all kept going

CHAPTER 20
MY 40ᵀᴴ ANNIVERSARY CELEBRATION

The following year was the fortieth anniversary of the founding of The Drifters. I was the Guest of Honor at a private reception hosted by Governor Carroll Campbell at the state mansion. From there we went to the big event that I had planned at the Exhibition Center in Sumter on May 14, 1993. Many wonderful people came to celebrate with me, and I was happy to see fellow entertainers there to perform.

My friend Marv Johnson, perhaps best know for his Motown hit "You've Got What It Takes", gave an outstanding show. But when he finished performing, he came off stage and collapsed into Ray Peterson's arms. We were all very concerned as they took him to the hospital. We learned later that he did not survive. Everyone who was there agreed that his final performance was astounding.

MARV JOHNSON

L TO R: SOUTH CAROLINA SUPREME COURT
JUSTICE ERNEST FINNEY JR., SOUTH CAROLINA
GOVERNOR CARROLL CAMPBELL, BILL PINKNEY

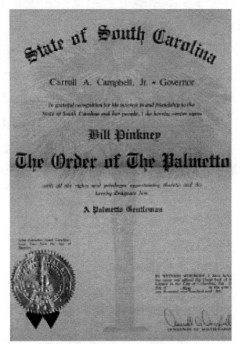

ORDER OF THE PALMETTO

Harry Turner wrote:

"I emceed Bill's 40th Anniversary with 'Rocking Ray' Gooding from WBT-AM radio in Charlotte. Supreme Court Justice Albert Finney, South Carolina Governor Carroll Campbell, Comptroller General Earle Morris, television personality Joe Pinner, wrestler Ric Flair, and other VIP's attended. Governor Campbell gave Bill the highest State civilian honor, the Order Of The Palmetto.

"Despite the concern about Marv's collapse [unknown to the audience], the air seemed electrically charged that night. It was a fitting tribute to the last original Drifter. Before the event, Bill had been hinting about retirement. Afterwards, he confided me to me, 'Well Harry, it's been some kind of 40 years. Guess it's time for me to start on 40 more. I got to keep going and stay active.' That was some of the most beautiful Drifiters' music I ever heard."

- - - - -

In June of 1993, I was invited and attended the groundbreaking ceremony for the Rock and Roll Hall of Fame and Museum in Cleveland, Ohio. It was a great interaction of many old friends.

Over the years, I had called the Atlantic Recording Company often, but Ahmet, Jerry, and the others were never available to take my calls and no one ever called me back. I felt I was due some royalty money. I wasn't getting any pension or health credit because the record company did not report to the union, so the union had not set up any account for me. They kept reproducing records I had recorded though. My voice showed up over the years on CDs in stores, on the soundtracks of movies, in commercials, and later on the internet.

We were working on a cruise ship in 1993. Sam Moore was working on the cruise too. I was made aware of a lawsuit that was being filed about some pension money and health benefits. I was asked to be involved as an artist from the fifties who never received either one. I was interested in anything to help me get some benefits.

That is how I became one of fifteen plaintiffs who sued the major record companies and the American Federation of Television and Radio Artists over heath and pension benefits.

The others were Barbara Acklin, Jerry Butler, Lester Chambers, Carl Gardner, Damon Harris, Brian Hyland, Doris Jackson, Curtis Mayfield, Sam Moore, David Prater, Jr., Marshall Thompson, Brenton Wood, and the Estates of Jackie Wilson and Mary Wells. The case dragged on for years. We eventually settled with the union in December 2002, but the issues with the record companies remained open.

- - - - - -

I was present for the grand opening of the Rock and Roll Hall of Fame and Museum on September 7, 1995. Seeing my signature on the Hall of Fame was almost like the first time I heard "Money Honey" on the radio. I thought of how proud my parents would have been.

MARY WILSON AND MRS. LOUIS (MARTHA) JORDAN

CHAPTER. 21
THE GOSPEL CALLING

Here are words from Bill Morris:

"Bill Pinkney, my brother, my friend. I can first recall those magical sounds of The Drifters in the early 50's when I first attended pre-teenage parties that ushered me from grammar school to my junior high days. That was the moment when the music became an indelible part of my heart and the very essence of the memories that I treasure today.

"It was in Oxford, Mississippi in the spring of 1963 at a sorority formal that I met Bill Pinkney back stage. The Drifters were performing at Ole Miss and I just had to meet the people that had given us the music. There was Bill Pinkney changing from a red tuxedo into a white one during intermission getting ready for his second show. I can still recall him hopping around on one leg trying to get his leg in his trousers as he was telling me about himself. Our visit didn't last long but the memories of that experience did until 1985 when The Drifters were performing again in Jackson, Mississippi.

"It was an icy winter night in which the city of Jackson had been virtually paralyzed. I still do not know how they were able to get in here - but they did. We took a serious chance in trying to get out to the Hilton where they were performing. I had no idea that it would be Bill Pinkney's group. The second I heard the harmony I realized that it was the real thing. I went up and saw that Bill was there. During a time in which they came out into the audience singing they would alternate the mike between the lead singer and any brave soul who would be willing to try and hit a few notes. I did not need much of a dare for I joined in with them as they did one of The Impressions' famous songs 'I'm So Proud'. People later told me that they thought I had been rehearsing with the group and that it had been prearranged. It was not.

"During a break I went over and acquainted myself with Bill Pinkney. I began to tell him about my
experience with Prentiss Barnes, The Moonglows'
original bass singer, and his heart began to jump.
He said 'Do you know Prentiss Barnes?' I said:
'He is a very dear friend of mine and lives here in
Jackson.' He asked if I would take him to see
Prentiss. In fact, I arranged to pick up Prentiss
the next day and took him down to the Ramada
Coliseum where Bill was staying. I will never forget when Bill and Prentiss, who had not seen each
other for many years, embraced one another. Bill
put his big, burly arms around Prentiss and said:
'Oh, Prentiss brother! I have missed seeing you!'
It was all I could do to keep from tearing up. It was
a grand moment for me and for them.

"From there we went into Bill's room. I listened to
Bill and Prentiss talk about old times at The Apollo
Theatre and Carnegie Hall and about movies that
they have been in and the good and bad experiences that they had. Bill wrote on the back of an
envelope all of the singers and various persons
that were still with the early famous vocal groups
that had formed the music that made our lives.
He asked me to see what I could do to get Dick

Clark to recognize all of them. I told him that I would do what I could. That three hours together was the basis of the deep friendship that goes on today.

"I wrote to Dick Clark and he later responded, but his show for the upcoming fall was absolutely set. As so many times has been the case; unfortunately, it did not include the real pioneers. He mainly had secondary people that came along in the 60's and later.

"In thinking back on my visit with Bill and Prentiss I had the warmest feeling of a significant moment. I said to myself that I would have given anything to be able to record (it). I remember saying: 'God, if you'll ever give me another chance to do that I will not pass it up'."

- - - - -

We were in Vicksburg, Mississippi for a weekend at the Ameristar Casino in August, 1994. Bill Morris called and later brought Prentiss Barnes to visit. We had a joyous reunion that afternoon. Bill taped the two of us talking about the way it was way back then. We spoke of so many old friends, many gone now, who never got their just due because of the record company practices. But we recalled some high points too, because we had many of those.

Since they weren't able to stay for the show that night, we ended that visit in a circle of prayer. Matthew 8 says, "Where two or more are gathered in My Name, I will be in the midst". As Bill prayed, the Holy Spirit filled my suite and everyone could feel that something greater was happening.

Before they left, we took a bunch of pictures in the parking lot. We promised not to lose touch again. But then, it was time to start getting ready for showtime.

Near the end of the first show, the sound engineer began to speak.

> *"Mr. Pinkney, Ameristar Casinos welcomes you and your fine act to Ameristar Casino Vicksburg. We are pleased to have you as a part of our corporate entertainment roster, and we extend sincere greetings to you on your 69th birthday."*

Before I could respond, Frankie Griffin, our opening act female vocalist at the time, and Maxine rolled out a cart carrying a huge beautifully decorated birthday cake and champagne onto the stage. I was surprised and moved. I felt truly Blessed. I switched songs on my band and closed the show with the hymn "I Need Thee Ev'ry Hour".

When we finished performing that night, I had a surprise celebration in my suite with family and friends. Maxine had ordered food and Eartha and Marchelle had decorated everything, including the windows. And I enjoyed it so much!

BILL PINKNEY WITH PRENTISS BARNES

SINGER TONI WILLIAMS, MARCHELLE, EARTHA, AND
SINGER FRANKIE GRIFFIN SHARE A BIRTHDAY SONG

A short while later, Bill Morris sent Maxine copies of pictures taken that day. She called to thank him, told him about the experience he had missed, and shared a copy of her partial show tape. He was so moved that he said, "If he ever decides to do a gospel album, I'll produce it". We didn't know then, but this was the birth of "Peace in the Valley" by The Original Drifters featuring Bill Pinkney. The liner notes begin "Born of a prayer in a motel room".

My group recorded it at Blackberry Records' McComb, MS studio. Doug and Melvin Williams of The Williams Brothers, renowned gospel artists, produced it.

With the rest of us, Doug joined on the last part of "Amazing Grace", and Melvin joined in on the end of "Just Drifting Along", a song Clifford Curry wrote for me. Paul Porter of The Christiannaires wrote "That's Why I Love Him So" and shared the lead on it.

There was one song that had Ali Woodson's name written all over it. Maxine located him on tour with The Temptations in Connecticut and called him about the project. He wanted to be a part of it, so she coordinated a release from Motown Records. He flew down to record "True Love" and nailed it

The CD also included "Just a Closer Walk With Thee", "Blessing Me", "What A Friend (We Have In Jesus)", "I Feel the Lord Walking With Me", and the title song. I recorded "White Christmas" again. The producers recruited The Mississippi Chorus to do the background singing with us on "America The Beautiful". Of course, I sang "I Need Thee Ev'ry Hour", the one that inspired the album, and one of the songs my mother used to sing.

But I'll let Bill Morris tell it:

"Well, sure enough, as God is faithful, He did give me another chance. It was just a few years later in the mid 1990's that I read where Bill Pinkney and The Original Drifters would be performing at the Ameristar Casino in Vicksburg. I called Prentiss and asked him to come with me to see Bill. That Saturday morning we went over. In fact, it was Bill's 69th birthday. Bill had a suite at the Delta Point Inn overlooking the mighty Mississippi River.

"It was also my first time to meet the lovely Maxine Porter who is Bill's business manager.

"Bill, Prentiss, and I began to reminisce once again. This time I did not miss the opportunity to record it. I began to hear the same conversation going on except my ears perceived one additional thing. Every time Bill would get to a certain point he would say: 'You know, God has been so good to me' and Prentiss would respond: 'Yes He has. He has been good to me too!' That one-hour conversation became so spiritual that I turned off the recorder and said: 'I feel the Holy Spirit instructing us to pray.' So there the four of us held hands and prayed in that motel room together. I did not know what was intended, but I felt God's hand upon us. I knew that something mighty would come out of it.

"About two months later I received a call from an insurance company (about) a band for their upcoming convention in Cancun, Mexico. I said that I knew just the people – 'How about The Original Drifters?'

"They were very interested and asked to hear something recent. I had a copy of the show when we had prayed earlier in that day, his birthday. I listened to it recalling the fabulous sounds of Bill's Original Drifters.

"There was one other thing, however, that happened on that tape at the end of the performance. Bill Pinkney asked the audience: 'Folks, God has been so good to me, would you mind if I close this show with a gospel number?' The crowd responded with loud applause and Bill began to sing 'I Need Thee'.

"As I drove to the office listening to this, tears began to come down my cheeks and I knew what was being asked of me. It was the answer to what happened in the motel room back in August. Bill and I agreed to pray about a gospel CD for a couple of months and if we both get a 'yes', I'd put him in touch with the people to do it.

"Sure enough, in Cancun at the insurance convention we put the deal together. Little did I know that I would soon become president of Hallelujah Productions, Inc. I also enjoyed doing the lead on a song with The Original Drifters that I have done many times since with them – 'Daddy's Home.'

"When I got back to Jackson, Mississippi I called Mike Frascogna. Mike said 'I've got just the people that can help us produce it. My clients

"The Williams Brothers own Blackberry Records
and they are one of the nations top stars and producers in black gospel music.' The deal was
done. We met with Bill and he brought his group
to Jackson for the production. As I recall, it took
almost three different occasions to complete what
we were doing, but we had 12 fabulous gospel
songs which also included a couple of other famous secular songs 'America, The Beautiful' and
'White Christmas'.

"Bonnie Raitt came within an eyelash of doing a
song with Bill but their schedules were too com-
plicated to get together at the time. Wynona Judd
also considered it but she was in the throws of
some things in her personal life that did not allow
her to do it.

"We released 'Peace in the Valley' in July of 1996.
It got a huge amount of play to begin with but, as
is sometimes the case with so many things in the
field of music today, the distribution did not get
done right. We re-released it under (another
song) title "True Love", led by the incredible Ali
Woodson, formerly of the Temptations.

"The CD is truly one of the best compilations of music that I have ever heard. I do not say that as the president of Hallelujah Productions or as one of the executive producers. I say it because out of nearly 1,500 CD's in my collection, I consider it one of the best. The music never gets old. One can listen to it over and over and over and still want more. I believe that God put this music together for a purpose and it will be seen in due time. Since that time Bill Pinkney's Original Drifters have performed more and more in the gospel setting.

"One of the things that developed in this process was a deep and abiding mutual friendship that Bill Pinkney and I have. Each time we talk we get a glowing feeling. God is always in the center of our discussions. Bill told me about a miracle experience that he had about three Christmases ago when he received a significant healing of a physical ailment that had been plaguing him.

"Bill and I have been together on many happy occasions. The most recent was his performance for the inaugural event of This Magic Moment, a fund I established under the auspices of The Com-

munity Foundation of Greater Jackson, Mississippi to benefit singers like Prentiss and others
with financial needs but no resources to respond
to them. I wanted the entire Jackson community
to be a part of that, and they were.

"Bill came in for the performance even though that
Friday morning he was in the doctor's office because of the pain in his lower back and legs. He
could only stand for a minute or two before he
would have to sit down. My priest and I prayed
over Bill a great deal before that performance and
it came off mightily.

"Also, Harvey Fuqua, Prentiss Barnes (our first
honoree) and Reggie Gordon of The Magnificents
came in to be a part of this. Harvey and Reggie
came in at their own expense and Bill donated
his Original Drifters' time at a greatly reduced
price. They all wanted to honor their brother
Prentiss. The incomparable Rufus McKay, the
original lead singer of The Red Tops Orchestra,
came in and thrilled the audience with his memorable rendition of 'Danny Boy'. Some there had
paid $1,000 to hear him perform that once again.
I even got to do my rendition of "Daddy's Home',
and what a joy and privilege it was.

"My memories of Bill also go back to so many of his birthdays and other times that we have been together with gatherings of great friends, musicians, and singers who have come to pay tribute to this great man. Bill is without question one of my very best friends and certainly one of the nicest blessings that God has given me in my life. The thought of him and the friendship that we share blesses me. I think also of all who love him like I do and of how he has honored God with the love that he has for other people and that they have for him. May he be blessed for years to come and still regale us with his wonderful sounds of The Original Drifters as they keep 'drifting along'."

I was thankful for the opportunity to record an all gospel CD because gospel is my roots and I love it so much. I have been asked how I could be a Christian and sing in nightclubs? I answer very sincerely "If you're a Christian when you go in, you'll be one when you come out". You never know who you'll touch when you let God use you.

God provides, and I knew my bread and butter was where I had been using my God-given talent. It was time to start moving again, but now we would be available for gospel concerts too.

While not on tour with my Original Drifters, I performed with the gospel group "The Traveling Echoes."

CHAPTER 22
MORE LEGAL ISSUES

This would be a very, very long chapter if lawyers were writing it. But this is my story, as I lived it and how I felt about and understood the legal comings and goings, so it is a short chapter.

So many things were happening on the legal scene that I couldn't keep up with them. I really didn't understand why I should have any legal problems at all since I had been doing the same thing since the fifties – pleasing the public and earning an honest living, while trying to treat people right. I had to trust my lawyers to do the right thing and to act in my best interest.

The Atlantic City case was not finished, with my money still on hold. I finally prevailed, but the money paid some legal fees. Marshak filed lawsuits in different states about advertising, each suit basically the same , and expensive to defend. The Federal Court in Charlotte, North Carolina consolidated all of the cases, and we resolved them in 1996.

While that case was pending, something interesting happened. I learned that the 1950's former manager's widow had a 1970 Default Judgment against my use of "The Drifters or The Original Drifters". As my lawyers dealt with that, I got a Court Order that allowed me to "…continue conducting (my) business activities as (I) had heretofore been doing…", and a later Court Order that reversed the Default Judgment. This action opened the door to use of both "The Drifters" and "The Original Drifters". Later, I won on Marshak's appeal in a decision in which the Court fined both him AND his lawyer for "frivolous litigation".

Meanwhile, "generic Drifters" were showing up all over the country, sometimes in three different places at the same time, using the name of our legacy established in the fifties, with no authentic contributor involved. The presenters appear only interested in making money. They deceive the public with no guilt and no legal problems.

I like Maxine's comparison. She said:

"If I go into a store and buy a can of Coca Cola, I expect just that in the can. When I pour the liquid into a glass, it should not be clear like 7-Up or Sprite. If it is clear, I did not receive what is on the label. That is consumer fraud."

"Likewise, generic acts should be billed as a salute, tribute, or some like moniker, to avoid the public inference that original and / or recording artists are performing. Some of those imposters even go so far as to say in their show that 'we recorded ...' or '... one of our hits.'

"Those imposters bask in reflected glory. When the dust from the rhetoric settles, it is public deception, plain and simple."

- - - - -

It didn't seem right to me. I kept going in spite of it all.

3 BILLS - BILL BAILEY, BILL PINKNEY, AND BILL RU-
THERFORD - HOLDING 3 COPIES OF BILL
PINKNEY'S "WHITE CHRISTMAS"

CHAPTER 23
THE MID NINETIES

The Beach Music scene is very much alive in the south-eastern United States and up the Atlantic coast. Drifters music, old and new, is very popular there, and we work a good bit in the area. In 1991, *Move Across the River* was number one on the beach charts for months and was the Song of the Year at the Cammy Awards. I received the 1995 Lifetime Achievement Award, the 1998 Best R&B Collaboration Award for a remake of the 1955 *Steamboat*, and the 1999 Joe Pope Pioneer Award.

Harry Turner gave this overview in *This Magic Moment:*

"In the Carolinas when R&B began to be referred to as beach music in the early 1970's, it cemented the connection between the music and the South Carolina coast. At that time beach music signi-fied only R&B, most of which one could shag to.

But the rush was on by competing shag DJ's to find new or obscure material to play. Enterprising individuals began to repress records. Sometimes it was done legally from the original master, other times it would be bootlegged from a clean 45. Many of the artists never got a penny from new pressings. It's hard to break the endless circle when money is involved.

"As beach music grew in popularity during the 80's, there were a couple of disturbing developments. Dancers began shagging to country and western, disco, and pop music records, in addition to R&B as long as they contained the mandatory 120 beats per minute. The dance began to dictate the music rather than the other way around. The shag is one of the only dances to have drifted away from the music from which it was spawned. What had made the dance so irresistible was its musical R&B roots and the fun times the music afforded.

"About the same time, regional horn bands began to supplant the original artists. It disturbed me to see groups who had never had anything other than regional hits, get concert billing over artists with national hits, like the Tams - simply because they were the right color, good looking, and had the right connections. Just as Elvis and the Beatles took the play away from the black R&B singers in the 50's and 60's, so too have imitators in the Carolinas since the 70's.

"Still beach music reigns supreme in the Carolinas. There have been biannual S.O.S. Shagging events since the early 80's that draw thousands of shaggers from all over the country to North Myrtle Beach. Shaggers become teenagers all over again, reliving the glory of the early days. Shag clubs literally dot the landscape in the Carolinas and have been spreading to other neighboring states. Beach music charts are updated periodically. There have been four Carolina beach music awards show, three televised nationally.

"My old favorites have continued to perform in the Carolinas. Many a time, I have seen a sign advertising Bill Pinkney and the Original Drifters, the Clovers, Maurice Williams and the Zodiacs, and Swinging Medallions, Billy Scott, Clifford Curry, Archie Bell, or the Tams, and my car has come to a screeching halt."

- - - - -

While I am respected greatly as a performer in the beach music market, I don't think that I see the kind of royalties that the popularity of our newer recordings justifies. But the beat goes on, and I go on.

FIRST MEMBERSHIP IN THE CAROLINAS
ROCK 'N ROLL HALL OF FAME

RUDY SINGLETON SPEARHEADED THE
EFFORT TO CREATE BILL PINKNEY PARK

THE MONUMENT READS:
WILLIE (BILL) PINKNEY PARK
DEDICATED OCTOBER 25, 1996
BY THE CITIZENS OF SUMTER COUNTY
THE STATE OF SOUTH CAOLINA
AND THE NATION

We traveled to Japan in February of 1997 to perform at the American Embassy and at military bases. My old friend Jim Vose spearheaded the effort to insure that my group was the one who performed at the club that he managed at Yokota Air Force Base north of Tokyo.

He contacted Tokyo promoter Cap Gaspar, who called Las Vegas agent Lee Maynard, who got in touch with Maxine. "The rest is history". We were well received and invited back for longer six months later.

Maxine still often recalls the trip and the evening at the Embassy where there was such a feeling of being "at home" on a holiday with the best china, linen, silver, and crystal. We were impressed by the respectful nature and dignity of the Japanese people.

In March of 1997 agent John Villano of JP Productions booked us at the Foxwoods Casino in Ledyard, CT. It was reputed to be the largest casino in the United States. My group shared the billing with The Coasters (Carl Gardner's group) and The Platters (Herb Reed's group).

John was very outspoken in his opposition to imposter acts who have no original or recording connection, but deceive the public by using the names of classic acts. He chose these acts to present a show containing an original recording member from each classic group. It worked – it was a knockout show, and the first time the three of us has shared the same stage together since the fifties. We have all performed together a number of times in various locations around the country since then.

About the legal front, Maxine shares the following:

"I guess it was inevitable that Marshak and Treadwell would fight it out. I'm not a lawyer, but this is the way I understand what happened.

"Faye Treadwell wrote the book 'Save the Last Dance for Me', in which she claimed to be the 'lawful owner' of The Drifters' name. Marshak, the mark holder, sued her because of that claim. After the legal wranglings, Treadwell prevailed in her claim that he obtained the mark by fraud, and Marshak prevailed in his claim that she abandoned the mark. Culminating in a late 1990's appeal, she prevailed on the abandonment claim. Pinkney, not a party to their litigations, filed a registration opposition with the U.S. Patent and Trademark Office."

BILL PINKNEY AND DICK CLARK AT THE AMERICAN
BANDSTAND 45TH ANNIVERSARY CELEBRATION

BILL PINKNEY PERFORMING THE AWARD WIN-
NING "RUBY BABY" AT THE 1998 CAMMY AWARDS
WITH THE SOFTONES.

CHAPTER 24
PEAKS AND VALLEYS

Carl Gardner's 70th birthday party in April 1998 was grand.
His wife Veta had planned an elegant dinner party and
show at Club Med. We shared a table with Peggy
Davidson of The Angels and her party.

Carl was a member of The Sharps, who later became
The Coasters. Also a part of the '50's, they had big hits
with "Yakety Yak", "Along Came Jones", "Searchin'", and
"Charlie Brown". Carl's healing from throat cancer was
more reason to celebrate.

Guest artists, family, business associates, and friends -
many from miles away - came to sing and celebrate. Our
attorneys Lawrence E. Feldman and James E. Slattery
also attended. Many artists offered musical selections.
That was a great evening and I was very happy for Carl.
You see, God only promised us threescore and ten.

- - - - -

The next month, Dr. Mom passed away. She had been hospitalized, but I didn't realize how low she was. When I called on Mother's Day, Maxine told me that Mama seemed to be really failing fast, but it was still a shock to me to receive the call when she passed two days later. She had been like a Mother to the entire Original Drifters family, as she treated us like her own, and she always took the time to share words of wisdom with earch of us. She called me her Son.

I went to Vegas for the service there, and flew back with Maxine to take Dr. Mom back to her hometown, Toledo, Ohio. Her entire Original Drifters family boarded my tour bus - the "Team Bus" - to participate in the Homegoing service in Ohio.

"In this life, we don't come here to stay. We're just passing through."

- - - - -

STROM THURMOND
South Carolina

COMMITTEES
ARMED SERVICES, CHAIRMAN
JUDICIARY
VETERANS' AFFAIRS

PRESIDENT PRO TEMPORE
UNITED STATES SENATE

United States Senate
WASHINGTON, DC 20510-4001

May 28, 1998

Mr. Bill Pinkney
Superstars Unlimited
P. O. Box 371371
Las Vegas, NV 89137

Dear Mr. Pinkney:

Thank you for your letter concerning the application of trademark laws to recording artists.

I believe that intellectual property is one of the most important aspects of the American economy. I believe that creators should receive reasonable support and remuneration for their works.

In the House of Representatives, Congressman Dennis Kucinich is working to develop legislation in order to deal with the issue you explained in your letter. In this regard, hearings were held in the House of Representatives on this matter in the Intellectual Property Subcommittee of the House Judiciary Committee on May 21, 1998.

Thank you for bringing this matter to my attention. I appreciate having the benefit of your informed views and will keep them in mind as this issue is further considered in the Congress and specifically in the Senate Judiciary Committee.

With kindest regards and best wishes,

Sincerely,

Strom Thurmond

ST:gm

LETTER FROM SENATOR STROM THURMOND
ADDRESSING MY CONCERNS ABOUT "NAME USE" LAWS

State of South Carolina

Presents to

Bill Pinkney

this

Certificate of Commendation

*for his contributions to the field of Arts & Entertainment and for the example he has set
for people throughout America by exercising his Christian values.*

May 21, 1998
Date

David M. Beasley
Governor

ARTS AND HUMANITARIANISM AWARD FROM
GOVERNOR DAVID BEASLY

We were on an engagement at the Hondah Casino way up in the mountains in Pinetop, Arizona in late July. As the week went on, I could feel myself feeling worse each day. By the end of the engagement, I felt terrible.

Maxine tried her best to persuade me to get medical help there. Even at the airport, she tried to get me to take the one hour Vegas flight with her instead of the long one back east. She wanted to call her doctor for immediate attention when the flight arrived. I insisted on heading back and just made it home and fell into bed.

A friend, Abraham Alston, just happened to come by the house. He told me to get up and immediately took me to Dr. Joe Williams. When the doctor walked in to the examining room and took one look at me, he called the Tuomey Medical Center and reserved a bed.

I knew I was sick, but I had no idea that I had double pneumonia. A few days later, I had complete heart failure. The fast action of the doctors there at Tuomey Hospital, with God in charge of course, kept me here. He must have kept me here for a reason.

- - - - -

After a few weeks when I got stronger, I went back out on the road again - just a little bit slower, sitting on a stool sometimes, thankful be able to do what I love, spreading a positive message.

We performed near Tampa area in late September. Our next show was in Naples two days later, but Hurricane Andrew caused the whole convention to be cancelled.

This brings us up to the point where I started this book – the Vocal Group Hall of Fame inaugural class induction in October. Thinking back to where I had been just two months earlier, I had good reason to shed tears of joy.

We got back to Toledo family and friends in December of 1998 for a more pleasant reason than seven months earlier. Maxine's cousins Eddie and Henrietta Burks had the group over for a down home dinner. We performed at the Stranahan Performing Arts Center on a show with Sam Moore, The Crystals, Freddie Cannon, and Brian Hyland. This time we were able to enjoy Toledo.

CHAPTER 25
PIONEER AWARD

The Rhythm & Blues Foundation was ten years old. As Chuck Jackson had said the first year: "A lot of guys never got theirs. What they got was like drippings from a beehive full of honey. What we're trying to do here is attack the beehive and get some of the *real* honey".

They had always acknowledged that The Drifters from both eras had a major presence in music history and an impact on the industry. Both Clyde McPhatter and Ben E. King had received solo honors, but it was understood that the unspoken underlying recognition was as Drifters contributors first and foremost.

They cited possible legal problems from the mark holder of "The Drifters" name as a reason for not having given recognition to other contributors to the legacy. Over the years many Artists had taken the stage to receive their awards mentioning The Drifters, and some me by name, as their mentors and / or influences.

In late 1998, a foundation staff member called my office with the news that my personal recruit Johnny Moore, Charlie Thomas, and I had been voted for individual 1999 Pioneer Awards, but would share the compensation as a group. For legal reasons at the time, they would not use The Drifters name, nor would they have us sing on the program. They called me on tour to notify me.

TRIO'S PUBLICTY PHOTO -
BILL PINKNEY, JOHNNY MOORE, CHARLIE THOMAS

I spoke with Johnny and Charlie by telephone. We all looked forward to seeing each other. Our anticipation was dampened on receiving the news that Johnny passed away in England in December 1998, just two months before the event. We were saddened even more to learn that he would not be funeralized and buried in America.

My daughter Eartha accompanied me on my flight and Maxine met us at the Los Angeles airport. We went by limousine to the Wyndham Bel-Age Hotel. When we entered the lobby, I saw and introduced my party to some of my old friends in the business coming and going – members of The Manhattans and the Blue Belles, and Joe Simon.

We met Mrs. Johnny (Judy) Adams and their daughter Alitalia, there to receive Johnny's award. We liked them right away and "adopted" them. Judy was determined to see her late husband get his *just due.*

We settled in and checked the schedule. Since the Pioneer Awards were a part of the Grammy Week activities, we had many activities to consider. We attended a gospel Grammy party and enjoyed an evening of good old-fashioned gospel music.

At the press party the next afternoon, microphones were thrust at all of us, with the honorees answering questions and posing for photos. Gladys Knight tried to enter the room, but she was so swamped by the press at the door that she didn't stay, graciously saying that it was a day for the honorees.

Charlie Thomas and I got a lot of attention from them because it was such a *long time coming*. The reporters had little tact, and got "to the meat and potatoes" of the issues.

On the big evening while we awaited limousines, I spotted many old friends that I hadn't seen in years. We shared a limo with Dee Dee Warwick and her party. The reception setting was lavish, with a delicious buffet. Maxine had a chance to visit with her friend and sister Links, Inc. member, Claudette Robinson of The Miracles.

Then we moved across the street for the big event in a huge tent on the Sony Pictures Studios lot in Culver City. My brother Murry's granddaughter Teresa Nixon, an actress who lives in Los Angeles, joined us to complete my foursome.

Smokey Robinson was a great emcee. A real who's who attended - artists, record label executives, writers, producers, and many fans and friends. I really missed my long time friend Ruth Brown, who was responsible for the Foundation's existence, absent due to illness.

Many of the people in town for the Grammy Awards stopped by. Lauryn Hill, who had just received five

Grammys, came to honor Patti LaBelle & The Bluebells and to show her respect in general. She expressed a very special thank you to all of the Pioneers "on whose shoulders we stand" on behalf of all younger artists. "You are personally responsible for our success".

Judy Adams, with her daughter standing with her, accepted her late husband's award with a warning for all artists. She called recording companies' practices as "slavery in a suit" and she advised artists loudly to RUN, not walk, to a good lawyer. Later in the program, Bonnie Raitt commented, "All you record company people here, you sell their music, pay them their money."

After the presentations, some of the honorees sang their signature song. Since Charlie and I had not been invited to sing with the orchestra, he just broke into "Under the Boardwalk" impromptu when we received our award. I joined in to give him some background vocals as the orchestra began to play it, and the audience clapped a wonderful beat. After that, Johnny's widow and two children accepted his award.

Patti Labelle & The Bluebells (with Sarah Dash, Nona Hendryx, and Cindy Birdsong) came together for the first time in thirty years and sang "You'll Never Walk Alone".

The Manhattans (Gerald Alston, Blue Lovett, Kenneth Kelly, and Sonny Bivins) sang "Kiss and Say Goodbye" after a hilarious introduction by comedian Sinbad. Barbara Lewis sang "Hello Stranger" and Brenda Holloway sang "Every Little Bit Hurts". Ashford and Simpson turned the house out with "Solid As A Rock". Other honorees were Joe Simon ("Drowning In My Own Tears"), Garnett Mimms ("Cry, Cry, Baby"), guitarist / songwriter Mickey Baker (of Mickey & Sylvia's "Love Is Strange"), Dee Dee Warwick (receiving her award from big sister Dionne), Barbara Lynn, and the song-writing team David Porter and Isaac Hayes.

The late Sam Cooke received the first annual Legacy Award, and John Lee Hooker was honored with the Lifetime Achievement Award. Eric Clapton, Bonnie Raitt, Kevin Eubanks, and Larry Graham joined John Lee Hooker on stage for a jam session to top it off. It truly was a night to remember for all of us, and a mountaintop experience for me.

I was on a 7:00 a.m. flight the next morning heading to Miami for a performance that night.

PIONEERS BILL PINKNEY &
CHARLIE THOMAS

CHAPTER 26
MOUNTAINTOPS

Speaking of mountaintops, I went to Capitol Hill that April to lobby Congress on behalf of original and or recording artists who have trouble working. Mary Wilson, Sam Moore, Peggy Davidson, Joe Terry, Carl Gardner, Charlie Thomas, Dee Dee Kenniebrew and others participated. We want Congress to pass laws that protect the public from deception and insure that the artists who created the music can earn a living from those efforts.

Many artists can't work because they never understood the need for legal protection or, if they understood, they found out too late or didn't know how to get it. Many others can't work because there are many impostor groups using the same or similarly confusing names. Most generic acts don't have any connection to the legacies they try to represent. We need to deal with the legal loopholes that allow this.

Dennis Kucinich, D-OH, and Charlie Norwood, R-GA, sponsored the bipartisan "Truth In Rock" bill. I think it's good to have organizations like Friends Against Musical Exploitation (F.A.M.E.) and the Truth in Rock Association committed to addressing this cause. I encourage my fans and friends to support efforts of this kind.

- - - - - -

Another mountaintop experience was in May when we taped the Circle of Friends Reunion for television. We recorded it over a period of two days at Studio 56 Productions, a Hollywood vintage recording facility.

I especially enjoyed the theme and the fellowship with other original artists. Each of us sang one or two of our known hits and then a gospel favorite, and we discussed how the gospel – and our faith - had affected our lives and our careers. I sang "Ruby Baby", "Money Honey", and my favorite gospel song "I Need Thee (Ev'ry Hour)". When I got finished, they asked for one more. "Precious Lord" just came to me, and I sang it from my heart.

The other participating artists were were Rosa and Barbara Hawkins (Dixie Cups), Dee Dee Kenniebrew (Crystals), Herb Reed (Platters), Carl Gardner (Coasters), Dave Sommerville (Diamonds), Barbara Lewis ("Hello

Stranger"), Bruce (Four Preps), Jewel Aikens ("The Birds and the Bees"), Brenda Holloway ("Every Little Bit Hurts"), Paul and Paula ("Hey Paula"), Ray Peterson ("Tell Laura I Love Her"), and Dennis Yost ("Classics 4"). Bob Duncan (Diamonds) was a very sincere and capable host.

- - - - -

South African President Nelson Mandela surprised me on my anniversary with a congratulatory letter.

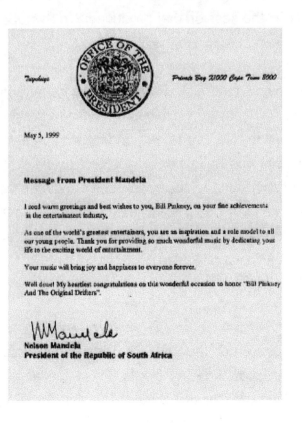

The Rock and Roll Hall of Fame filmed my oral history to add to its Legends Series permanent archives in 2000. I appreciated the good treatment and respect paid by Ruthie Brown, the Community Programs Director, who coordinated it. Maxine joined me for the filming. We enjoyed dinner at Morton's with Ruthie, her husband Bill, who has family in South Carolina too. While having dinner, I ran into my old friend, Mickey Baker, who had come over from England, and who received a Pioneer Award on the same night that I did. He had played that sweet guitar on the session that produced "No Sweet Lovin'" when we recorded it in the 50's.

Early the next morning, Ruthie and the cameraman arrived. We spent almost five hours with few breaks, talking about my life, my career, and the rhythm and blues music that was the foundation for Rock and Roll. It's real American history. I hope people see it and hear the truth about the early days, not from the many well-meaning researchers who usually spell my name wrong, but from the one who actually lived it.

- - - - -

We appeared on the NBC-TV Today Show broadcast from the Boardwalk in Atlantic City in July as a part of their Summer Concert Series. We flew into Philadelphia and traveled by limousine from there. The folks at Trump Plaza treated us royally while we were lodged there. We were on the Boardwalk between Caesar's Palace and Trump's for a sound check at 5:00 a.m. the next morning. The show aired at 7:00 a.m., and we had to sing our first song at the beginning of the show. We sang "Money Honey", "Up On The Roof", "Under The Boardwalk", and "White Christmas" (yes in July – as I sometimes have to do at concerts year round). I took Greg Johnson and Richard Knight Dunbar from my group and welcomed Drifter Charlie Thomas joining us as a special guest.

We enjoyed working with the Today Show staff. Katie Couric was so personable and very genuine when she emphasized our introduction The ORIGINAL Drifters. My band members took plenty of pictures with her. We missed the weatherman Al Roker and the co-host Matt Lauer, since when we were on-location. We'll just have to meet them next time.

We went to San Jose, California for the City of Hope fundraiser at the San Jose arena in August, in concert with The Beach Boys and Jerry Lee Lewis – all Rock and Roll Hall of Fame members. Bill Graham Presents was coordinating the show, and Epicentro Marketing

Services handled our arrangements. We heard they did very well for the charity. That always makes me feel good.

We were off to Vegas to celebrate my 74th birthday the next day. When the limousine came for me, I was surprised to find Carl and Veta Gardner. I had no idea they were coming from Florida. We went to an elegant reception at Sun City Summerlin's Desert Vista, arriving to concert pianist Emilo Morrell's live music.

Journalist Pete Allman announced Carl's arrival, and then my arrival escorted by Veta. We enjoyed good music and food, and I got a lot of very thoughtful birthday presents. I was thrilled to see Mildred Ward Coffey there with her brother Vernon Ward who came from California. Their oldest brother Leon had been one of my very close friends.

After the reception, everyone moved to the Starlite Theater a few blocks away for an intimate concert. I received plenty of presents and surprise letters from President Bill Clinton and Las Vegas Mayor Jan Jones. Lou Ragland of the World Famous Ink Spots and Jimmy "Fashion Plate" Payton helped Maxine with the planning.

BILL WITH FRIENDS MILDRED WARD COFFEY AND
VERNON WARD

WITH CARL AND VETA GARDNER

We went on to spend a week in Jackpot, Nevada at Cactus Pete's Resort Casino. I have enjoyed annual engagements there for more than a decade, and we always look forward to returning there and to the other corporate properties.

Veterans' Day found us in our nation's capitol for the Disabled American Veterans annual gala. As a fellow veteran, I was honored to provide the entertainment in support of the national heroes. I, too, was showered with much appreciated respect as a fellow veteran.

Beverly Hills, California is beautiful during the Christmas season. We performed at the Museum of Television Arts and Science for We The People. Besides the magnificent sights, we enjoyed the Regent Beverly Wilshire Hotel too.

We brought in the year 2000 in Cincinnati. With all of the millennium hype, everybody expected "something to happen." The hotel even gave out souvenir flashlights "just in case." Since there was no year 00, it seemed to me that we should have celebrated it the next year at the end of 2000, but we still celebrated right along with everyone else.

CHAPTER 27
KEEPING GOING AT 75

My 75th birthday celebration was the most memorable one that I ever had. Maxine worked tirelessly for months long distance coordinating the event that she named "Experience the Evening", a private formal banquet with a five course dinner - with guests roasting me afterwards, and then a public concert. She chaired the Jubilee Roast Eleganza, and Harry Turner chaired Legends Concert. My friend Dee Dee Kenniebrew of The Crystals was the Mistress of Ceremonies, and well-known radio announcer Andy Thomas was the Master of Ceremonies.

"Downtown" Ruthie Brown, not to be confused with Ruth Brown, supported her "homegirl" Maxine representing the Rock and Roll Hall of Fame. Billy Scott represented the Cammy Awards. Others on the dais were Bill Morris, Hallelujah Productions, and Maxine's friend Renate Paxton who traveled the farthest from Frankfurt, Germany.

The special guest artists who attended were The Dixie Cups (Barbara and Rosa Hawkins), The Doo Wop Royal All Stars (Artie Loria, Eugene Pitt, Harold Washington, Danny Loria), Harvey Fuqua (The Moonglows), Danny and the Juniors (Joe Terry, Frank and Robert Maffei), Gloria Jones (formerly with The Shirelles featuring Doris Jackson), William Guest (Gladys Knight & The Pips), and The Legendary Orioles.

Harry Turner gave a short greeting and introduced the hostess. Maxine presented the occasion, citing me as an Entertainment Industry Living Legend and a National Treasure, and introduced me. I was escorted to the dais amidst a memorable, warm, long, and loving applause.

I was a proud veteran as we stood for the Presentation of the Colors by an Honor Guard from the Fort Jackson, Army Base in Columbia, SC. After introductions of the dais, Bill Morris gave the invocation, and we enjoyed the fine dinner, complete with the cake and birthday song.

Then they got the roasting started with remarks from the sponsors. Al Wicenski, representing Jay Spector of Insurall Casualty Group, recalled listening to early Drifters music while he served in Vietnam in the late '60's, and spoke about a statewide television commercial I had done for them a few years before. Bill Kovacs from Mid-point GMC Dealership in Rocky Mount, Virginia talked about my love for old cars. When I would perform in his area, I often stopped by his business and asked what he had on the back line that was real cheap.

My great niece, Teresa Nixon, came from Los Angeles to represent my family. Calling me a great role model with "will power and spunk", she spoke of our supportive family and how they often traveled with me. She said, "I have come to honor your crown, embellished with hope and trimmed in love".

Chuck Cockerham represented The Original Drifters family, recalling many years on the road, saying that the group felt privileged to "grace the stage" with me because I love what I do. Speaking of the ups and downs of touring, he said "sometimes we call him 'Dad', sometimes we call him 'Pop', and sometimes things got so tough out there we called him things I can't tell y'all".

Bill Morris spoke in depth about the first time he saw me performing in Jackson, Mississippi in 1963 at "Ole Miss" and then talked about the prayerful reunion thirty years later that led to "Peace in the Valley".

My friend Harvey Fuqua of The Moonglows came forward not to roast, but calling me "a great guy all the way around" and choosing to give a prayer thanking God for "raising us above the distinction of evil men". Moved, Maxine referred to Harvey and me as "Elder Statesmen".

Billy Scott, Cammy Awards President, did a "Papa Was a Rolling Stone" parody. He called me his inspiration, noting that I always believed in being on time. He recalled a trip to Kissimmee, Florida in the 80's to support For the Love of Rock and Roll, an organization that Joey Dee of the Starliters, Dee Clark, and other artists were working with to preserve the music of the fifties and sixties. Harry Turner had been dropping hints all during the trip that Billy would be a "good Drifter, wouldn't he Bill?" Billy ended by saying "I always wanted to be a Drifter".

Ruthie Brown recalled the time earlier in the year when she coordinated my oral history filming for the Rock and Roll Hall of Fame, calling it a "highlight" of her career. She said I taught her how to be asked fewer questions by taking an hour and a half to answer each one.

Maxine spoke beautifully on how pleased she was to be present in three capacities. She publicly thanked me for making a difference in her life by opening doors to many new personal and professional opportunities, and for my teaching the entertainment business to her. Then she officially delivered a Proclamation by Governor Kenny Guinn from my second home state, Nevada. It got even better when she floored me with a replica forty year over due Gold Record for "White Christmas".

Broadcaster and former Presidential candidate Alan Keyes sent a warm letter saying that I reminded him of his father Alison L. Keyes, an Army Command sergeant in the Korean War. The letter reads in part:

> "My Father, like you, loved this land, despite her imperfections, and always stood strong in all aspects of your life and forged ahead with dignity, honor, and steadfast integrity.

> "From…baseball…to your decorated service during World War II to the happiness you have brought to millions with your music, you have been sustained through your unwavering devotion to God and Country. You are truly a National Treasure."

The final speaker was Alan Freed Foundation President Tony Belmont, who spoke of touring in the fifties along with Jackie Wilson and Dee Clark. He recalled when Shirley Alston Reeves of the Shirelles asked, "What time do The Drifters eat"? Tony told her 7:00 pm and asked her why. "So the girls and I can eat at 6:30 pm. If those Drifters get there first, there won't be any food left!"

After the laughter died down, Tony then surprised me with a letter from President Bill Clinton, which read in part:

> *I am pleased to recognize the many contributions of a great American on his 75th birthday. Bill, you served in the Army with distinction and bravery, were awarded multiple Bronze Stars and a Presidential Unit Citation, and returned a genuine American hero.*
>
> *Many would have felt that we had accomplished enough good in life. But not you. Providence had ordained much more for your life. You gave us some of the greatest music in the world – it's American history.*
>
> *For your outstanding military career I salute you. For the wonderful music that has given us all great memories, I applaud you. You are an inspiration.*

I felt particularly honored by the President's words.

I wouldn't have missed a minute of it. I was too full to say much when asked to have expressions at the end, but I did tell everyone that I truly appreciated them and that it was all by God's Grace and to His Glory. In closing, I told them that if I didn't live to see another birthday, I was happy. "This is the way I want to leave you – with joy".

DINING WITH THE HOSTESS

LETTER FROM
PRESIDENT CLINTON

DEE DEE KENNIEBREW,
ROSA HAWKINS, AND
BARBARA HAWKINS SING
AT LEGENDS CONCERT

WITH WARLENE GLENN
AT CONCERT

JOE GIGANTI (CENTER) JOINS DOO WOP
ROYAL ALL-STARS DANNY LORIA, ART LORIA,
EUGENE PITT, AND HAROLD WASHINGTON

BILL MORRIS

BILLY SCOTT

RUTHIE BROWN AND TONY BELMONT

WITH TOMMY ELLISON

DEE DEE KENNIEBREW AND ANDY THOMAS,
MISTRESS AND MASTER OF CEREMONIES

DANNY AND THE JUNIORS (FRANK MAFFEI,
ROBERT MAFFEI, AND JOE TERRY)

THERESA NIXON

HARVEY FUQUA

- - - - - -

My bus hit the road the next day for New Orleans. We went to the Gospel Music Workshop of America to debut a gospel CD "Fire", recorded on my Pinkney Records label at Bradley House Studio in Quinby, SC. I decided to rename it "Fire is Coming" when it was picked up by Worldwide Gospel Music for a short while a bit later.

A Who's Who of Gospel was there. We fired them up with "It's Gonna Rain". I then told the audience I was thankful to God and "it took me 75 years to get here tonight". The house went up. I closed with "That Same Old Candle Light" and into "Blessed Assurance".

- - - - -

Three days later, I took my group to support Ben E. King at his annual Stand By Me Foundation golf tournament and concert to provide arts scholarships. We went to the Lansdowne Country Club in Leesburg, Virginia. Benny and Charlie Thomas joined my group on stage and sang. It was the first time that the only three living Hall of Fame Drifters had performed together. We have always kept in touch.

In fact, Charlie Thomas performed with my touring group in the early 90's, including a two week Vegas engagement. He even stayed at my house for a while and went out golfing. We all are friends who respect and care about one another. There is no truth to the hype otherwise.

Many celebrities participated in the weekend festivities - The Dells, The O'Jays, The Teenagers, The Orlons, The Cadillacs, Maxine Brown, Gerald Alston, Blue Lovett, Gary U.S. Bonds, The Five Satins, The Four Aces, The Legendary Orioles, Danny and the Juniors, Fay Hauser, Beverly Crosby, Clifton Davis, Gary Hudson, Tommy Ford, Bobby Bennett, Louis Price, and, of course, Ben.

I felt honored that my fellow entertainers gave me the night's only standing ovation when, by request, I sang "White Christmas".

BILL PINKNEY, BEN E. KING, AND CHARLIE THOMAS
THE ONLY SURVIVING
ROCK AND ROLL HALL OF FAME DRIFTERS

CHAPTER 28
THE ELUSIVE VEGAS DREAM

Ruth Brown and Maxine talked on the telephone every once in while, just keeping in touch. Ruth asked her to tell me that, if I ever needed a good tenor, her son Ronnie, who was Clyde McPhatter's son, was the one for the job. He played the part of The Platters' original lead singer Tony Williams in the movie about the life of Frankie Lymon, "Why Do Fools Fall in Love". We kept him in mind.

In June, 2001, a promoter called Maxine with a Las Vegas engagement extended offer. I had considered relocating to Las Vegas, but I had to be able to make a living out west because I had no pension or medical benefits.

We began making fast plans. Because I already had eight singers who I rotated and the full band, I planned to

take just three singers. The other singers would stay with
the band and fulfill the dates on the book.

Maxine contacted the people on the upcoming itinerary
and made special arrangements for my absence with
most of them. I would have to fly back for a few, but she
had cleared this possibility in advance with the new promoter.

I flew to Vegas in July for a few days. Maxine and I had
lunch with the promoter and his wife, and I toured the
venue. She finalized the negotiations, arranged for air-
line tickets, and found apartments for the guys. Everything on the Vegas end appeared to be all set to go.

Meanwhile, I closed down my South Carolina house and
listed it with a realtor. People seemed to be genuinely
happy for me. I received a congratulatory letter from
Governor Jim Hodges wishing me well.

- - - - - -

I arrived in Vegas first.

I had spoken by telephone with Ron David McPhatter,
and I had heard some of his music. I decided to hire him

because I wanted to present a five man front line show. We arranged a meeting that night.

As we waited in the lobby at New York New York Hotel & Casino, I asked Maxine how will we know him. She said, "Let's just wait and we'll see", and then just moments later "There he is". Since I couldn't see him from the angle where I was sitting, I asked her how she knew it was him. She said, "Because he looks like Clyde".

Then I saw him and his mother. I saw his father's good looks and bright smile. It was just like going back in time. He was a winning combination with two great Rock and Roll Hall of Famers as parents. He was personable, like his parents, and had a good voice too.

Later I saw him perform with a local group. I almost saw Clyde on stage again. It was almost prophetic that Clyde's son should be with me as I carried The Original Drifters' legacy into the new millennium.

It was a wonderful reunion for my old friend Ruth and me. After the hellos and big hugs, we all grabbed a bite to eat and had a good visit. We went across the street to the MGM Grand Hotel & Casino to see comedian George Carlin perform.

A staunch fifties music lover, George welcomed us back-stage after his show. He seemed genuine and delighted to meet us. He talked about all his old music that he had that Ruth and I didn't have. He promised to share it with us. He was a man of his word. He sent them to us just as he promised. And we appreciated that.

My singers Chuck Cockerham, Richard Knight Dunbar, and Vernon Young arrived later arrived later in the week. We got the guys settled into their furnished apartments and got them a rental car.

They came over to practice new routines and to have dinner every day. Because Maxine had traveled so much with us over the years, they did not know what a great cook she is. Everybody found out then, and the guys loved the attention.

We got musician Woody Woods to write new musical arrangements for us, and secured renowned choreogra-pher Cholly Atkins to work up new routines. We spent the next two days rehearsing with Cholly.

Everything was perfect …
                              and then the bottom fell out.

- - - - - -

On Thursday evening, the promoter called with the hotel's corporate legal counsel on the conference call. They had received a letter and some telephone calls from a Joe Vincent. He threatened litigation citing a defunct Court Order and a "registered trademark" that the U.S. Patent & Trademark office had not registered. Everyone knows that hotel/casinos are considered "deep pockets" and are frequent targets. Because the hotel was already involved in a lawsuit about an act that contained no original and/or recording members, they would let us open without clear legal documents to refute what they had received.

I could tell from the look on Maxine's face that something was seriously wrong. She was frozen for a moment, and then she shifted gears. She got our counsel on the call too. He explained it as best he could. Unfortunately, it was going to take time to search very old files to provide the documents. We didn't have the luxury of time.

The hotel press hit the Friday morning newspapers with a beautiful color advertisement. The show opened on Friday with what they called "a temporary replacement" to fill in until we addressed the legal issue.

- - - - -

My 76th birthday the next Thursday didn't go unnoticed. I had a great brithday dinner party.

Sonny Turner (The Platters), my Goddaughter Arlene, our friend and attorney Paul Sorenson with his daughter Chelsea (who calls me her "Uncle Bill"), the church family, my guys - some past and present- Rev. Alexander and Wanda Cotton, Cecil Davis, Eagle Eye Shields, Marian and Pitt Burns, along with neighbors, joined in to pack the house for the festivities and fellowship.

My Godson Ali-Ollie Woodson (who started on the road with me) brought his family. As the evening came to a close, he sang a capela "I Won't Complain" and "I Feel Like Going On". It was an enjoyable intimate birthday celebration.

BILL PINKNEY WITH CRAIG RUCKER M.D.

BILL PINKNEY WITH SONNY TURNER

BILL PINKNEY WITH ALI WOODSON

- - - - -

We prayed about the job, and we worked feverishly for the next month trying to get the necessary documents and support for the hotel so that we could salvage the date. The law firm I had used before no longer existed. It took a while to locate one of the attorneys, now in his new Charlotte, North Carolina office. He told us that all of the records from the previous firm were archived in the Atlanta office of another firm. It would take time that we did not have to get whatever records they had.

We even tried to negotiate an agreement with another promoter who was willing to take the necessary legal steps to protect potential interest relating to licensing my name/mark for limited use elsewhere. That didn't happen however.

That's when September 11th, 2001 totally sideswiped us. With the rest of the world, we sat in front of the television and watched in disbelief. The world was changing forever before our eyes.

On the business side, Las Vegas revenues and visitor counts nose-dived, and our hopes did too. But we kept trying. We kept the faith.

That two-month period cost a lot in relocating and getting situated. It took almost two more weeks to accept
that it must not be God's plan for us to stay just then. We
had to go back east where the work was. After all, we
already had quite a few jobs on the book.

And you have to keep going in life.

BILL PINKNEY WITH RON DAVID MCPHATTER

CELEBRATING JESSE STONE'S 100TH BIRTHDAY
ANNIVERSARY IN ORLANDO, FL. ON 11/16/01 - BIIL,
MRS. JESSE (EVELYN MCGEE) STONE & TOM DOWD

JANUARY 2002 - LAS VEGAS, NV
SONNY TURNER (PLATTERS), BILL, AND
CARL GARDNER (COASTERS)

CHAPTER 29
2002

2002 was a busy and interesting year. We brought in the New Year at the Jubilee Casino in Greenwood, Mississippi. Friends drove all the way from Texas and Alabama. I had a special feeling about that night. I knew I was Blessed to see another year.

- - - - - -

Shortly after the first of the year, I finally saw some results from our long-fought legal battle over pension and health benefits. As these things seem to go, you never see what you think you really should, but I have learned to look at things in a positive way. The bottom line is that it's more than I had.

- - - - -

Time-Life released the Special Edition *Rock & Roll at 50* listing "The Top 100 Rock & Rollers of All Time". The Drifters were right there at number 19. Only one Black group, The Miracles listed at number 13, ranked ahead of us. I was really pleased that they chose to include an early Drifters photograph of Bubba, Gay, Little Dave, and me – The Original Drifters after Clyde was drafted – with guitarist Jimmy Oliver. I am proud of the part that I played in starting it and in keeping it alive.

- - - - - -

Another highlight for me was performing for the National Baseball Hall of Fame and Museum's Players Reunion during the induction weekend of superstar Ozzie Smith. Jane Forbes Clark really knows how to make people feel welcome in Cooperstown, New York. Mike Carney, yes Art's nephew, handled every detail insure a great show.

The athletes were excited to meet me, calling me a true legend. I was complimented and just as excited. I was pleased to meet them as legends too. What they didn't realize is that, just like my music entertained them over the years, it was their baseball games that entertained me for years in those hotels and motels along the way.

Forty eight of fifty eight living Hall of Fame members were in for the weekend festivities – and I tried to meet them all. Stan Musial played his harmonica with us. Yogi Berra, Rod Carew, Bob Gibson, Dave Winfield, Billy Williams - they were all there! Closing with a gospel tinged medley of "America the Beautiful" and "Battle Hymn of the Republic", it seemed as if my life had come full circle to the gospel music I sang and the baseball I played in the 40's and 50's. What a night! I felt honored!

WITH ROD CAREW

STEVE CARLTON

WITH YOGI BERRA

WITH 2002 INDUCTEE OZZIE SMITH

THAT'S STAN MUSIAL ON HARMONICA
ACCOMPANYING THE ORGINAL DRIFTERS BAND

WITH DAVE WINFIELD

WITH BOB GIBSON

- - - - - -

Ronnie McDowell asked my group to be part of his new CD and video project in the summer of 2002. We had done some touring with him in the previous couple of years. Ronnie, a serious Drifters fan who is well known in the country music arena, did a great job recording some '50's songs and some new material with us. That just goes to show you how music can unite worlds.

The CD is getting good early reviews. Who knows? Just like the young people of today still seek out "The Original Drifters" sounds from the fifties, years from now, I hope that young people will still be listening to my present group, "Bill Pinkney's Original Drifters," too.

- - - - - -

In addition to road travel, our extended contract with Royal Caribbean International lets us relax a little, while continuing to meet new people, see many old friends, and still spread a good message.

2003 VOCAL GROUP HALL OF FAME INDUCTION CONCERT

CHAPTER 30
2003 - MY FIFTIETH ANNIVERSARY

I remember my old friend Brook Benton (Ben Peay) telling me, "You get happy once you realize what it is all about." While it has been a year with some medical challenges, I am happy as I enjoy the 50th Anniversary of when we formed The Drifters in 1953. And I intend to celebrate August 9, 2003 for an entire year with book signings, touring, and whatever else God has in store.

It is hard to imagine that it has been fifty years. None of us realized that it would last so long or the impact that we would have on the music industry. I feel just like a proud parent, pleased to present shows that reflect the entire Drifters presence in the music industry, and I appreciate the respect and recognition that I receive.

I have looked back quite a bit this year. I thought about Buddy Holly, that skinny kid from Texas, jumping on the table and saying, "If my friends can't eat in here, we're all leaving." Now that was a civil rights stand.

I recently did some reflecting with my legal counsel Lawrence E. Feldman. Larry has been there through most of the legal battles since the late 1980's, and he still is working with me to right some of the wrongs that happened over the years.

Chuck Jackson and I talked about a gig in the 60's at the Eastwood Country Club in San Antonio, Texas. Chuck had a brand new white Chrysler LeBaron just like Dinah Washington's blue one.

My old war buddy Berkley Porter passed this year. We had sung together in the 40's, talked together, laughed together, enjoyed life together, and stayed in touch over the years.

My niece Helen reminisced about my Mama's cooking. Mama was such a great cook, and we would have the food every day that most people just had on Sundays.

I get a lot of mail from www.originaldrifters.com, my Internet website. I recently heard from a man who re-membered seeing my group with Wayne Cochran & The CC Riders in Missouri about thirty five years ago during a two month tour. He commented that Wayne had a bottle of Tequila in one hand and a bottle of vodka in the other. Actually, it was a part of the act at the time. Wayne is a minister now.

I heard from Margo & The Marvettes who toured with Gay, Bobby Hollis, Bobby Hendricks and me back in 1966 in Germany.

I love hearing from people. It is so good to be remembered and to have people write to say, "I saw your show in . . . " or just a meaningful "thank you for the Music."

- - - - -

I am often asked about my thoughts on the music business today. I think it is good that the young artists don't have to face the hurdles that we pioneers faced. We paved the way for them. Unlike us, today's artists know more about how the music business works and they are able to protect themselves and what they create.

It is sad that some express themselves in a negative way and with disrespect toward women. While I don't think that they mean any harm, I am concerned about the effect that the language could have on young minds and their outlook on the future.

Yet there are many who have a positive message for the young generation.

I can't predict what's going to happen, but I really would like to see the young artists carry on the rhythm and blues tradition, following in the footsteps of the Drifters and other music pioneers.

- - - - -

Sometimes I "look back and wonder how I got over," especially in my later years without pension and health benefits. And I wonder what is just and right for me - a seventy eight year old man who has spent the last fifty years on the road doing the only thing I know how to do. I just hope I live long enough to get my "just due."

But I am thankful that God has allowed me to have so many wonderful experiences. To receive an honorary doctorate from Coastal Carolina University, to see a park named in my honor on the land near where I was born, to receive commemorative coins from three Four Star Generals (Lester Lyles, Bill Eberhardt, and B. Bell), to enjoy receiving so many other honors and awards, and to carry on a great legacy. He has healed my body from illness more than once and has been so good to me.

I intend to keep on doing what I have been doing, *Just Drifting Along*, for as long as God gives me the health and strength to do it. Then I still want the music to stay alive and keep going. I plan to leave a strong legacy of perseverance, responsibility, humanitarianism, and faith.

Through it all, and above everything else,
I have remained thankful . . .
And I have kept my promise
to Clyde to keep it alive , , ,

THE DRIFTERS - 1953
CLYDE MCPHATTER (STANDING), BILL PINKNEY, GERHARDT
THRASHER, WILLIE FERBEE, AND ANDREW THRASHER

THE ORIGINAL DRIFTERS - 2003
BILL PINKNEY (FAR RIGHT) WITH (L TO R)
VERNON YOUNG, RON MCPHATTER, CHUCK
COCKERHAM, AND RICHARD KNIGHT DUNBAR

BILL PINKNEY WITH MAXINE PORTER

EPILOGUE

Bill Pinkney's professional contributions and honors are many. He has donated countless performance hours supporting law enforcement and substance abuse awareness throughout South Carolina. Area school children visit him and tour his home on annual Black History Month field trips. He received the legislative Jean Laney Harris Folk Heritage Award and the United Black Fund Award, and was profiled in the state's African American History Online and included on a BellSouth historical calendar.

Bill's group performed on the acclaimed Public Broadcasting System television special *Doo Wop 51,* filmed in 2001 and chronicling America's Golden Music. He acknowledges producer T. J. Lubinsky, a young man whose love for music made him go back and bring up many almost forgotten Artists to entertain a new generation.

The accolades for Bill Pinkney continue. North and South Carolina have included him in their states' Music Halls of Fame, and the latter commissioned him the State's official "Ambassador of Entertainment".

The "Entertainment Capital of the World", Las Vegas, proclaimed the "ORIGINAL DRIFTERS Day" and "BILL PINKNEY Day" in honor of his respective fortieth and forty-fifth anniversary kickoffs. South Carolina and Nevada, his home state and second home state, proclaimed "Bill Pinkney Day" on August 15, 2000 honoring his 75th birthday. South Carolina and Texas legislators entered Congressional Records, and Mississippi, Indiana, and Ohio issued proclamations. He holds the keys to many cities, including Las Vegas.

Bill Pinkney keeps going - a real testament to survival. As he enjoys more recognition for his exemplary life and the sole designation for his fifty years representing the Original Drifters legacy, I am thankful that he has had many opportunities to "smell the flowers." I wish him a prosperous, healthy, and happy Fiftieth Anniversary year and more, filled with Blessings as he continues "Just Drifting Along."

- Maxine Porter

JUST DRIFTING ALONG

I've been traveling this road for so many years
I've been up and down through laughter and tears
I've made a lot of friends along the way
I thank the Lord every day
Just drifting along singing my song,
 I'm just drifting along singing my song

I've been north and south, east and west
I sang for so long without no rest
But I can't stop now, I've got to be strong
I've got to keep rolling on
Just drifting along singing my song,
 I'm just drifting along singing my song

By bus, by car, by plane and train
In hotels and motels, so insane
I love to hear the roar of the crowd
Making them happy makes me feel so proud

So I'll keep on travelling from town to town
People come out and hear the original sound
I want to thank my many fans and friends
Stick with me until the end
Just drifting along singing my song,
 I'm just drifting along singing my song
- Clifford Curry

QUOTES FROM FRIENDS & FANS

"Imitators and one hit wonders will always come and go. But the real pros of the music business will always be around because they have a special, rare talent. You can't keep the cream from rising to the top." – *Barry White*

"Clyde McPhatter and Bill Pinkney were, like wow! They were the ultimate group. Everybody wanted to be like them." – *Lou Rawls*

"Steamboat (sung)! I love you Bill. God Bless you. A beautiful man and a beautiful group." – *James Brown*

"Just keep on keeping on Bill. I have loved your music forever. Good health, good wealth, love, faith, and prosperity." – *Marla Gibbs*

"Thank you. It's great to have people who paved the way for artists such as myself and so many more. You set such a good example. It's an honor even to do what I do knowing there are such great legends who have done it before me." – *Devante Swing (Jodeci)*

"Without you, the rest of us wouldn't be here."
– *Jim Fuller (The Safaris)*

"Happy Anniversary Bill. We love you and we appreciate you." – *Harry Elleston (Friends of Distinction)*

"Congratulations! I can't imagine what it would be like to be out there fifty years. That's classic music!"
– *Hawthorne James*

"I remember meeting Bill Pinkney in 1956 at the Apollo Theater. We were on a world tour together in the late 1950's visiting England, Scotland, Germany and Spain, with several groups. It included the Buddy Johnson Orchestra, the Drifters, Frankie Lyman and the Teenagers, the Platters, the Coasters, and our group the Heartbeats. Even with segregation rampant in those days, Bill was a gentleman. He has my greatest respect and love."
– *"Big John" Garfield (The Heartbeats)*

"Bill is the only living person I've known as an original Drifter. We went out with him and Gearhardt in '55 in North Carolina." – *Carl Gardner (The Coasters)*

"It was Bill Pinkney that kept the true Drifters sounds so much original. He is one of the true pioneers of the solid golden era who have given a lot to make their talents internationally known."
– *Paul "Billy" Wolfe (Sonny Til's Orioles)*

"Bill, it's like family when you are in the house."
– *Richard Nader*

"I had the pleasure of hearing The Drifters' Bill Pinkney's version, which is better than Bing Crosby's, live at the Vocal Group Hall of Fame's induction concert back in 1998. He walked through the crowd singing it a capella. Not a creature was stirring. Incredible."
– *Greg Loescher, editor, Goldmine Magazine*

"Bill, there's a young cat out here named John Salley whose brother made him clean all those records with just the right kind of cloth. Bless you. A lot of people come and go, but the real ones stay." – *John Salley*

"I had the pleasure of doing a number of gigs with my band backing up Bill Pinkney and the gang, and I confess there is not a nicer guy that I have met since in the business." – *Bill Cooksey*

"What an entertainer! I can't thank you enough for having remembered Jesse's 100th birthday. I had never seen you perform before. You're great.!!"
– *Mrs. Jesse (Evelyn McGee) Stone*

"(During my) childhood, we were all given joy and hope by the excellence of people most often made manifest to us through recorded music. Clyde McPhatter and The Drifters' 'White Christmas" was a jewel without peer."
– *Lawrence N. Redd, Ph.D., Michigan State University*

"What an excellent show, what a wonderful sound still after all these years. That man can move! Our hats are off to them." – *Vicki Wiesner*

"I still get goosebumps when I play *Warm Your Heart*."
– *Jack Strong*

"When I saw you perform recently, you brought tears of joy and warmth to my heart. My life as a 15 year old disc jockey on a local radio station in Rode Island was an enjoyable time because of your music. We all have prospered by you." – *Stan Hanson*

"Separation of the races – that is what America was at the time. But our parents were not able to stop us from falling in love with the music of The Drifters, Fats Domino, Laverne Baker, Ruth Brown, Joe Turner, The Clovers, Hank Ballard and the Midnighters, and so many others. I believe this was a major step in integrating America."
– *Ed Cullum*

"We love all your new songs, but the favorite is *Move Across the River.* Please keep on recording your great music for us to enjoy." – *Scotty Mack*

"Bill Pinkney has stood the test of time and his rewards have been long overdue. I have seen the electrifying performances of this quiet and humble man."
– *Obra Edgerton*

"The sparkle in your eyes still impresses me as you sing and entertain the world. God bless you friend. Keep playing the incredible music we love." – *Pat Gwinn*

SUGGESTED READING

Miss Rhythm
Ruth Brown & Andrew Yule
DaCapo Press; (April 1999)
ISBN: 0306808889

Yakety Yak, I Fought Back
"My Life With The Coasters"
An Autobiography
Carl Gardner

This Magic Moment:
Musical Reflections of a Generation
Harry Turner
A G M Enterprises; (May 1994)
ISBN: 096407611X

Supreme Faith: Someday We'll Be Together
Mary Wilson & Patricia Romanowski
HarperCollins; (October 1990)
ASIN: 0060162902

What'd I Say: The Atlantic Story
Ahmet Ertegun
Welcome Rain; (June 15, 2001)
ISBN: 1566490480

ACKNOWLEDGMENTS

The authors are deeply appreciative to those whose shared writings and/or thoughts appear in the text; Ruth Brown, L. C. Cooke, the late Tom Dowd, Carl Gardner, Bobby Hollis, Chuck Jackson, Ben E. King, Reggie Kimber, Willie Massey, Rudy McPhatter, Bill Morris, Eliza Pearson, Berkley Porter, Tommie Price, Billy Scott, Charlie Thomas, Harry Turner, and Maurice Williams.

…and to all who have been a part of the journey…

PHOTOGRAPHY CREDITS

Inside portrait and Page 233 - Morgan's Photography
        (Las Vegas, Nevada)
Pages 20 (2 at bottom) and 24 - Berkley Porter
Pages 28 and 115 - James Williams
Page 63 and 99 (Ruth Brown) - Ruth Brown
Page 100 (Hank Ballard) - Bill Butts
Pages 219 and 235(Bottom) - Kimberly Brown,
        Collette Photography (Globe, Arizona)
Page 228 - Bill Morris
Page 236 (Bottom) - Barbara Johnson

50 YEARS OF MEMORIES

TOP LEFT:
RUTHIE BROWN

TOP RIGHT:
WITH HERB REED (THE PLATTERS)

MIDDLE:
MAXINE PORTER AND VETA GARDNER

BOTTOM LEFT:
SONNY TURNER (THE PLATTERS) AND
CARL GARDNER (THE COASTERS)

BOTTOM RIGHT:
WITH DR. MOM

FAMILY

MURRY PINKNEY JR

MURRY'S WIDOW
MILLIE

JACKIE MATHIS, JANET (HENRY'S WIFE), ELIZA
PEARSON, HELEN NIXON (MURRY JR.'S
DAUGHTER), BESSIE HAWKINS, HENRY, AND
ISIS (ELIZA'S GRANDDAUGHTER)

HENRY, ELIZA, BESSIE, BILL

FAMILY

RHONDA JEFFERSON

DOROTHY POWELL

EARTHA JOHNSON, MARCHELLE MASSEY,
DARRYL PINKNEY, WILLIE WOODS,
DEBORAH BARBER

CARLETTER WILLIAMS

LAKEISHA DAVIS

MILITARY TRADITION

WILLIE WOODS

RODDEY FRANKLLIN

ABRAHAM JOHNSON
(EARTHA'S SON)

JOE RAY MASSEY
(MARCHELLE'S SON)

ROCK AND ROLL HALL OF FAME

**BILL . . .
STILL JUST
DRIFTING ALONG**

INDEX

#

135th Battalion 18
3991st Regiment 18
3rd Army Division 18
519th Regiment 18

A

Abraham, Miss 11
Abrahm, Silas (Chookie) 26
Abram, Delia 9
Abramson, Herb 39
Acklin, Barbara 146
Adams, Faye 52
Adams, Judy 183,185
Adams, Walter 44
African American History Online 238
Aikens, Jewel 126,191
Ali, Muhammad 91
Allen, Dick 49,89
Allen, Nick 108
Allman, Peter 2,194
Alston, Abraham 179
Alston, Gerald 186,210
American Bandstand 174
American Federation of Television and Radio Artist 145
American Guild of Variety Artists (AGVA) 82-83
Ameristar Casino 150-151,155
Ames Brothers, The 4,71
Ames, Ed 4
Anderson, Benny 117
Anderson, Elec Sr. 11
Anderson, Robert 28

Brown, Ruthie 192,197,200,206,248
Bruce (Four Preps) 191
Bryant, James 33
Bryant, Rusty 97
Buddy Johnson Orchestra 242
Buford, Richard 15
Bullmoose Jackson Orchestra, The 44
Burns, Pttt & Marian 216
Burnstein, Eleanor 96
Butala, Tony 2
Butler, Jerry 146
Butts, Bill 247

C

Cactus Pete's Resort Casino 195
Cadillacs, The 210
Cammy Awards 174,197
Camp Kilmer 22
Camp Miles Standish 18
Camp Robinson 15
Campanella, Roy 91
Campbell, Carroll 141,143-144
Cannon, Freddie 180
Captain Bilbrow's 117
Capters, Deacon J.C. 28
Cardinals, The 61
Carew, Rod 223
Carey, Ezekiel 54,70
Carey, Jacob 54
Carlin, George 213-214
Carlisle, Ben 9
Carlton, Steve 223
Carney, Mike 222
Carolinas Rock 'N Roll Hall of Fame, The 170
Carter, Johnny 54
Castaways, The 95

E

F

Johnson, Eartha Pinkney 57,84,152-153,183,250
Johnson, Freddie 5
Johnson, Greg 193
Johnson, James "Wrinkle" 35
Johnson, John H. 15
Johnson, Marie 12
Johnson, Marv 112,141-142,144
Jones, Dub 68,135
Jones, Gloria 198
Jones, Jan 194
Jones, Jiggs 16
Jones, Louis 33
Jordan, Martha 146
Jordon, Ron & Peg 138
JP Productions 172
Jubilee Casino 221
Justice, Bill 79

K

Kelly, Kenneth 186
Kennedy, Billy 78
Kenniebrew, Delores (Dee Dee) 189-190,197,204,207
Keyes, Alan 201
Keyes, Alison L. 201
Kimber, Reggie 44,74,78,247
King, Ben E. 86,119,121-122,181,209-210,247
King of Hearts Club 90
King Pleasure 52
King, Rev. Dr. Martin Luther Jr. 88
Kirby, George 52
Kirk, Rev. H.W. 28
Knight, Gladys 183
Kovacs, Bill 198
Kucinich, Dennis 190

New York Yankees 95
Nixon, Helen 1,230,249
Nixon, Teresa 184,199
Nixon, Theresa 208
Norwood, Charlie 190
Nunn, Bobby 68

O

O'Jays, The 210
Oliver, Jimmy 44,53,89,222
O'Neal, Buck 91
Orbison, Roy 90
Orlons, The 210

P

Paige, Satchel 91
Palmetto, Order of the 143-144
Parisian Hotel, The 49
Pate, Johnny 5
Patterson, Lover 86
Patti LaBelle & The Bluebells 93,185
Patton, P.O. "Pat" 107
Paul and Paula 191
Paul, Les 119
Paul Revere and the Raiders 138
Paul Weston Orchestra 54
Paxton, Renate 197
Payton, Jimmy 194
Payton, Lawrence 71
Peake, Mary 79
Pearson, Eliza Pinkney 1,12,22,35,249
Peay, Benjamin. *See* Benton, Brook
Penguins, The 105
Penniman, (Little) Richard 67,79
Peoples, Bobby 117
Perkins, Roland R. 16